每天读一点英文

Everyday English Snack

那些给我勇气的句子

The words that encouraged me

章华◎编译

与美国人同步阅读的英语丛书
——美国英语教师协会推荐——

陕西师范大学出版社

图书在版编目（CIP）数据

那些给我勇气的句子:英汉对照/章华编译. —西安:
陕西师范大学出版社,2009.7
（每天读一点英文）
ISBN 978-7-5613-4725-6

Ⅰ.那… Ⅱ.章… Ⅲ.①英语—汉语—对照读物
②名句—汇编—世界 Ⅳ.H319.4:H

中国版本图书馆 CIP 数据核字（2009）第 105964 号

图书代号：SK9N0660

上架建议：英语学习

那些给我勇气的句子

作　者：章　华
责任编辑：周　宏
特约编辑：辛　艳　刘宇圣
封面设计：张丽娜
版式设计：风　筝
出版发行：**陕西师范大学出版社**
　　　　　（西安市陕西师大 120 信箱　邮编:710062）
印　刷：北京嘉业印刷厂
开　本：880×1230　1/32
字　数：200 千字
印　张：7
版　次：2009 年 7 月第一版
印　次：2009 年 9 月第二次印刷
ISBN 978-7-5613-4725-6
定　价：21.80 元

目录
CONTENTS

In grey dawn, the road to somewhere over the rainbow
灰色晨曦中，那通往彩虹的路

前行路上的 一盏灯
A lamp on the road

In Life, We are Happiest When...
生活中我们最幸福时

· Stuart ·

A man and his girlfriend were married. It was a large celebration. All of their friends and family came to see the lovely **ceremony** and to **partake** of the festivities and celebrations. All had wonderful time.

The bride was **gorgeous** in her white wedding gown and the groom was very dashing in his black **tuxedo**. Everyone could tell that the love they had for each other was true.

A few months later, the wife came to the husband with a proposal, "I read in a magazine, a while ago, about how we can strengthen our marriage," she offered, "Each of us will write a list of the things that we find a bit annoying with the other person. Then, *we can talk about how we can fix them together and make our lives happier together.*"

The husband agreed. So each of them went to a separate room in the house and thought of the things that annoyed them about the other. They thought about this question for the rest of the day and wrote down what they came up with.

The next morning, at the breakfast table, they decided that

they would go over their lists.

"I'll start," offered the wife. She took out her list. It had many items on it. Enough to fill 3 pages, in fact. As she started reading the list of the little **annoyances**, she noticed that tears were starting to appear in her husband's eyes.

"What's wrong?" she asked. "Nothing," the husband replied, "keep reading your list."

The wife continued to read until she had read all three pages to her husband. She neatly placed her list on the table and folded her hands over the top of it.

"Now, you read your list and then we'll talk about the things on both of our lists." She said happily.

Quietly the husband stated, "I don't have anything on my list. I think that you are perfect the way that you are. I don't want you to change anything for me. You are lovely and wonderful and I wouldn't want to try and change anything about you."

The wife, touched by his honesty and the depth of his love for her and his acceptance of her, turned her head and wept.

In life, there are enough times when we are disappointed, depressed and annoyed. We don't really have to go looking for them. We have a wonderful world that is full of beauty, light and promise. Why waste time in this world looking for the bad, disappointing or annoying when we can look around us, and see the **wondrous** things before us?

斯图亚特

一个男人与他的女朋友举行了一场盛大的结婚典礼。

所有的亲朋好友都来参加，分享他们的喜悦，对他们表示祝贺，大家过得很愉快。

身着雪白婚纱的新娘楚楚动人，穿着黑色礼服的新郎英俊潇洒。大家都看得出来，他们彼此相爱着。

数月后，妻子提议道："我刚在杂志上看到一篇文章，讲的是如何增进夫妻感情。"她说，"我们各自在纸上罗列出对方的小缺点，然后一起找出解决的办法，这样，会使我们的婚姻生活更融洽。"

丈夫很赞成。于是，他们各自在房间里想对方的缺点。那天余下的时间，他们都在想这个问题，同时也把所想的写了下来。

第二天早上，吃早餐时，他们决定谈谈彼此的缺点。

"我先来吧。"妻子说。她拿出单子，上面都写满了，足有三页纸。开始念丈夫的小毛病时，她注意到他的眼角湿润了。

"怎么了？"她问道。"没什么，"丈夫答道，"继续念啊。"

妻子接着念，念完这三张纸后，她把单子整齐地放在桌上，两手交叉放在上面。

"现在，该你了。你念完后，我们就来谈谈这些缺点吧。"妻子开心地说道。

丈夫平静地说："我什么也没写。我觉得你这样已经很完美了，你很可爱，很迷人，我不想让你为我改变什么。"

丈夫的诚实，深沉的爱与包容，深深地触动了她，她转过头去哭了起来。

生活中，很多时候，我们都会感到失望、沮丧和厌烦，但我们不必刻意去寻找这些负面的事情。我们拥有一个奇妙的世界，充满美、光明和希望。当我们环顾四周，就可以发觉这些美好，那又何必把光阴耗费在找寻不快、失落和烦恼上呢？

Practising
& Exercise

实战
提升篇

核心单词

ceremony [ˈserɪmənɪ] *n.* 仪式，典礼；礼仪，礼节

partake [pɑːˈteɪk] *v.* 分担；共享

gorgeous [ˈgɔːdʒəs] *adj.* 华丽的；灿烂的

tuxedo [tʌkˈsiːdəʊ] *n.* 男士无尾半正式晚礼服

annoyance [əˈnɔɪəns] *n.* 烦恼；可厌之事

wondrous [ˈwʌndrəs] *adj.* 令人惊奇的，非常的

实用句型

We can talk about how we can fix them together and make our lives happier together.

我们一起找出解决的办法，这样会使我们的婚姻生活更融洽。

①这里是 how 引导的宾语从句。

② talk about 谈论，谈到，类似的表达还有 talk with 与……交谈；talk over 商讨，讨论等固定搭配。

翻译行不行

1. 事实上，你这么做是对的。(in fact)

....

2. 他一时想不出一个合适的回答。(come up with)

....

3. 世界充满爱。(be full of)

....

Don't Work for Money
不做有才华的穷人

• Patty Hansen •

The world is filled with smart, talented, educated and gifted people. We meet them every day. A few days ago, my car was not running well. I pulled it into a garage and the young mechanic had it fixed in just a few minutes. He knew what was wrong by simply listening to the engine. I was amazed. The sad truth is, great talent is not enough.

I am constantly shocked at how little talented people earn. I heard the other day that less than 5 percent of Americans earn more than $ 100, 000 a year. A business **consultant** who specializes in the medical trade was telling me how many doctors, dentists and chiropractors struggle **financially**. All this time, I thought that when they graduated, the dollars would pour in. It was this business consultant who gave me the phrase, "They are one skill away from great wealth." What this phrase means is that most people need only to learn and master one more skill and their income would jump exponentially. I have mentioned before that financial intelligence is a synergy of accounting, investing , marketing and law. Combine those four technical skills and making money with money is easier. *When it comes to money, the only skill most people know is to work hard.*

When I graduated from the U. S. Merchant Marine Academy in 1969, my educated dad was happy. Standard Oil of California had hired me for its oil-tanker fleet. I had a great career ahead of me, yet I **resigned** after six months with the company and joined the Marine Corps to learn how to fly. My educated dad was devastated. Rich dad congratulated me.

Job **security** meant everything to my educated dad. Learning meant everything to my rich dad. Educated dad thought I went to school to learn to be a ship's officer. Rich dad knew that I went to school to study international trade. So as a student, I made cargo runs, navigating large freighters, oil tankers and passenger ships to the Far East and the South Pacific. While most of my classmates, including Mike, were partying at their fraternity houses, I was studying trade, people and cultures in Japan, Thailand, Singapore, Hong Kong, Vietnam, Korea and the Philippines. I also was partying, but it was not in any frat house. I grew up rapidly.

There is an old cliché that goes, "Job is an acronym for Just over Broke." And unfortunately, I would say that the saying applies to millions of people. Because school does not think financial intelligence is intelligence, most workers "live within their means". They work and they pay the bills. Instead I recommend to young people to seek work for what they will learn, more than what they will earn. Look down the road at what skills they want to acquire before choosing a specific profession and before getting trapped in the "Rat Race". Once people are trapped in the lifelong process of bill paying, they become like those little hamsters running around in those little metal wheels. Their little furry legs are spinning furiously, the wheel is turning **furiously**, but come tomorrow morning, they'll still be in the same cage: great job.

When I ask the classes I teach, "How many of you can cook a better hamburger than McDonald's?" Almost all the students raise their hands. I then ask, "So if most of you can cook a better hamburger, how come McDonald's makes more money than you?" The answer is obvious: McDonald's is excellent at business systems. The reason so many talented people are poor is because they focus on building a better hamburger and know little or nothing about business systems. The world is filled with talented poor people. All too often, they're poor or struggle financially or earn less than they are capable of, not because of what they know but because of what they do not know. They focus on perfecting their skills at building a better hamburger rather than the skills of selling and **delivering** the hamburger.

帕迪·汉森

世界上到处都是精明能干、才华横溢、学富五车以及极具天赋之人，我们每天都会见到他们。几天前，我的汽车运转不灵了。我把它开进了维修厂，一位年轻的机械工只用了几分钟就把它修好了。他仅凭倾听发动机的声音就能确定哪儿有毛病，这让我惊奇不已。然而遗憾的是，光有非凡才华是不够的。

我常常吃惊，为什么有才华的人却只有微薄的收入。前几天我听说，只有不到5%的美国人年收入在十万美元以上。一位精通药品贸易的商务顾问曾经告诉我，有许多医生、牙医和按摩师生活拮据。以前我总以为他们一毕业，财源便会滚滚而来。这位商务顾问告诉了我一句话："想发大财，他们还差一项技能。"这句话的意思是说，大部分人还需多学习并掌握一项技能，他们的收入才能呈指数倍增长。以前我提到过，财商是会计、投资、市场营销和法律方面的能力综合。将上述四种专业技能结合起来，以钱生钱就会更容易。说到钱，大部分人所知的唯一技能就是拼命工作。

1969年，我从美国海运学院毕业了。我那有学识的爸爸十分高兴，因为加州标准石油公司录用我为它的油轮队工作。尽管我的未来前程远大，但我还是在六个月后辞职离开了这家公司，加入海军陆战队去学习飞行。对此我那有学识的爸爸非常伤心，而富爸爸则为我做出的决定表示祝贺。

对于有学识的爸爸来说，稳定的工作就是一切。而对于富爸爸来说，学习才是一切。有学识的爸爸以为我上学是为了做一名船长，而富爸爸明白我上学是为了学习国际贸易。因此，在做学生时，我跑过货运、为前往远东及南太平洋的大型货轮、油轮和客轮导航。当我的大部分同班同学，包括迈克，在他们的联谊会会堂举办晚会的时候，我正在日本、泰国、新加坡、中国香港、越南、韩国和菲律宾学习贸易、人际关系和文化。

我也参加晚会，但不去任何联谊会，我迅速地成熟起来了。

常言道，"工作（job）就是'比破产强一点（Just Over Broke)'的缩写"。然而不幸的是，这句话确实适用于千百万人，因为学校没有把财商看作是一种才智，大部分工人都"量入为出"：干活挣钱，支付账单。相反，我劝告年轻人在寻找工作时要看看能从中学到什么，而不是只看能挣到多少。在选择某种特定职业之前或是陷入"老鼠赛跑（激烈的竞争）"之前，要好好掂量自己到底需要获得什么技能。人们一旦为支付账单而整天疲于奔命，那么就和那些在小铁轮里不停奔跑转圈的小老鼠一样了。老鼠的小毛腿跑得飞快，小铁轮也转得飞快，可到了第二天早上，他们发现自己依然困在同一个老鼠笼里，那就是：重要的工作。

当我在自己教授的班级上问到"你们当中有多少人做的汉堡包能比麦当劳更好"时，几乎所有的学生都举起了手。我接着问："如果你们当中大部分人都能做出比麦当劳更好的汉堡包，那为什么麦当劳比你们更能赚钱？"答案是显而易见的：麦当劳拥有一套出色的运营体系。许多才华横溢的人之所以贫穷，就是因为他们只是专心于做更好的汉堡包，而对运营体系几乎一无所知。世界上到处都是有才华的穷人。在很多情况下，他们之所以贫穷、生活拮据或者收入与其能力不相符，不是因为他们已知的东西而是因为他们未知的东西。他们只将注意力集中在提高和完善做汉堡包的技术上，却不注意提高有关汉堡包的销售和送货技能。

Practising
& Exercise

核心单词

consultant [kənˈsʌltənt] *n.* 顾问；会诊医生，顾问医生
financially [faiˈnænʃəli] *adv.* 财政上；金融上
resign [riˈzain] *v.* 放弃，辞去；把……托交给，委托
security [siˈkjuəriti] *n.* 安全，防备，保安
furiously [ˈfjuəriəsli] *adv.* 狂怒地；猛烈地
deliver [diˈlivə] *v.* 投递；传送；运送；发动

实用句型

When it comes to money, the only skill most people know is to work hard. 说到钱，大部分人所知的唯一技能就是拼命工作。
① it 在这里没有任何意义，只作形式上的成分。
② When it comes to 说到，类似的表达还有 speaking of 谈到；considering of 考虑到等固定搭配。

翻译行不行

1. 火车准时进站了。(pull into)

....

2. 他注视着我。(focus on)

....

3. 召之即来，来之能战，战之能胜。(be capable of)

....

What will Matter?
什么才重要?

· Bud Tenney ·

Ready or not, some day it will all come to an end. There will be no more sunrises, no days, no hours or minutes. All the things you collected, whether treasured or forgotten, will pass to someone else.

Your wealth, fame and **temporal** power will **shrivel** to irrelevance. It will not matter what you owned or what you were owed.

Your grudges, resentments, frustrations, and **jealousies** will finally disappear.

So, too, your hopes, ambitions, plans, and to-do lists will all expire. The wins and losses that once seemed so important will fade away.

It won't matter where you came from, or on what side of the tracks you lived.

It won't matter whether you were beautiful or **brilliant**. Your gender, skin color, **ethnicity** will be irrelevant.

So what will matter? How will the value of your days be measured?

What will matter is not what you bought, but what you built ; not what you got, but what you gave.

What will matter is not your success, but your significance.

What will matter is not what you learned, but what you taught.

What will matter is every act of **integrity**, compassion, courage and sacrifice that enriched, empowered or encouraged others to emulate your example.

What will matter is not your **competence**, but your character.

What will matter is not how many people you knew, but how many will feel a lasting loss when you're gone.

What will matter is how long you will be remembered, by whom and for what.

Living a life that matters doesn't happen by accident.

It's not a matter of circumstance but of choice.

Choose to live a life that matters.

巴德·坦尼

无论是否准备好,总有一天它都会走到尽头。那里没有日出,没有白天,没有小时和分钟。你收集的所有东西,不管你珍惜或忘记与否,它们都将流入他人手中。

不管是你得到的或是你欠别人的,可你的财产、名誉和权势也都会变成和你毫不相干的东西。

你的怨恨、愤慨、挫折和妒忌最终也将消失。

因此，你的希望、抱负、计划以及行动日程表也将全部结束。当初看得比较重的成功得失也会消失。

你来自何方，住在穷人区还是富人区也都不重要了。

你昔日的漂亮与辉煌也都不重要了，你的性别、肤色、种族地位也将消失。

因此，什么重要呢？怎么衡量你有生之年的价值呢？

重要的不是你买了什么，而是你创造了什么；不是你得到了什么，而是你给予了什么。

重要的不是你成功了，而是你生命的意义。

重要的不是你学到了什么，而是你传授了什么。

重要的是每个行动之中都有正直和勇气的气概，伟大的同情心和牺牲精神，并且鼓励他人遵从榜样。

重要的不是你的能力，而是你的性格。

重要的不是你认识多少人，而是在你离开后，别人会认为是个永远的损失。

重要的不是你想念谁，而是爱你的人想念你。

重要的是别人会记你多长时间，谁记着你，为什么记着你。

过一种有意义的生活不是偶然的。

那不是环境的问题，而是选择的问题。

选择有意义的人生吧！

Practising
& Exercise

实战
提升篇

核心单词

temporal ['tempərəl] *adj.* 暂存的，短暂的，世俗的；现世的

shrivel ['ʃrivl] *v.* 使束手无策；使无能为力；使无用

jealousy ['dʒeləsi] *n.* 妒忌；猜忌

brilliant ['briljənt] *adj.* 光辉的；优秀的；辉煌的；出色的

ethnicity [eθ'nisiti] *n.* 种族地位；种族特点；种族渊源

integrity [in'tegriti] *n.* 正直；廉正；诚实

competence ['kɔmpətəns] *n.* 能力，胜任，称职

实用句型

Ready or not，some day it will all come to an end．

无论是否准备好，总有一天它都会走到尽头。

①Ready or not是状语从句No matter you are ready or not的省略形式。

② come to涉及，达成，类似的表达还有come on进展，逐渐开始；come out 出现，出版；come up 开始，发生，被提出等固定搭配。

翻译行不行

1. 会议终于结束了。(come to an end)

....

2. 这不是你的错，而是他的问题。(not...but...)

....

3. 我偶然遇到了她。(by accident)

....

You're Awesome
令人敬畏的你

• Anonymous •

Consider...YOU. In all time before now and in all time to come, there has never been and will never be anyone just like you. You are **unique** in the entire history and future of the universe. Wow! Stop and think about that. You're better than one in a million, or a billion, or a gazillion...

You are the only one like you in a sea of **infinity**!

You're amazing! You're **awesome**! And by the way, TAG, you're it. As amazing and awesome as you already are, you can be even more so. Beautiful young people are the whimsy of nature, but beautiful old people are true works of art. But you don't become "beautiful" just by virtue of the aging process.

Real beauty comes from learning, growing, and loving in the ways of life. That is the Art of Life. You can learn slowly, and sometimes painfully, by just waiting for life to happen to you. Or you can choose to **accelerate** your growth and **intentionally** devour life and all it offers. *You are the artist that paints your future with the brush of today*.

Paint a Masterpiece.

God gives every bird its food, but he doesn't throw it into its nest. Wherever you want to go, whatever you want to do, it's truly up to you.

佚 名

试想一下……你空前绝后！无论过去还是将来都不会有一个和你完全一样的人。在整个历史和宇宙中。你也是独一无二的。噢！想想吧，你是一百万人、十亿人、一兆人中……最好的。

在浩渺的大千世界中，你绝无仅有！

你令人惊异！令人敬畏！没错，这就是你。生来不同凡响、卓越的你，还可以更加强大。美丽的年轻人是大自然的奇迹，美丽的老人是艺术家的杰作。而你却不会随着年龄的增长而自然变得"美丽"。

真正的美丽源于生命中不断地学习、成长和关爱。这就是生命的艺术。你可以选择等候命运的安排，缓慢地、有时甚至是痛苦地学习。你也可以选择使自己快速成长，如饥似渴地享用生活提供的一切。你就是用今天的画笔绘制未来宏伟蓝图的艺术家。

创作一幅杰作吧。

上帝给了鸟儿食物，但并未把它们扔进鸟巢。不论你想去哪里，要做什么，决定权在你自己。

核心单词

unique [ju:'ni:k] *adj.* 唯一的，独特的；无与伦比的

infinity [in'finiti] *n.* 无限，无穷大

awesome ['mɔːsəm] *adj.* 令人敬畏的；可怕的；有威严的

accelerate [æk'seləreit] *v.* 使增速；促进；促使

intentionally [in'tenʃənli] *adv.* 有意地，故意地

实用句型

You are the artist that paints your future with the brush of today.

你就是用今天的画笔绘制未来宏伟蓝图的艺术家。

① that 引导的定语从句在这里修饰限定 the artist。

② paint 即可作名词，也可作动词，类似的词还有 fool；knight；group；widow 等。

翻译行不行

1. 恰似你的温柔。(just like)

....

2. 凭借财富而行使权力的人。(by virtue of)

....

3. 你应该把实情告诉他。(want to)

....

Our Pursuit of Happiness
我们对幸福的追求

We chase after it, when it is waiting all about us.

"Are you happy?" I asked my brother, Ian, one day. "Yes. No. It depends on what you mean," he said.

"Then tell me," I asked, "when was the last time you think you were happy?"

"April 1967," he said.

It served me right for putting a serious question to someone who has joked his way through life. But Ian's answer reminded me that when we think about happiness, we usually think of something **extraordinary**, a **pinnacle** of **sheer** delight—and those pinnacles seem to get rarer the older we get.

For a child, happiness has a magical quality. I remember making hide-outs in newly cut hay, playing cops and robbers in the woods, getting a speaking part in the school play. Of course, kids also experience lows, but their delight at such peaks of pleasure as winning a race or getting a new bike is **unreserved**.

In the teenage years the concept of happiness changes. Suddenly it's conditional on such things as excitement, love, popularity and whether that zit will clear up before prom night. I can still feel the agony of not being invited to a party that almost everyone else was going to. But I also recall the ecstasy of being plucked from obscurity at another event to dance with a John Travolta look-alike.

In adulthood the things that bring profound joy—birth, love, marriage also—bring responsibility and the risk of loss. Love may not last, sex isn't always good, loved ones die. For adults, happiness is complicated.

My dictionary defines happy as "lucky" or "fortunate," but I think a better definition of happiness is "the capacity for enjoyment." The more we can enjoy what we have, the happier we are. It's easy to overlook the pleasure we get from loving and being loved, the company of friends, the freedom to live where we please, and even good health.

I added up my little moments of pleasure yesterday. First there was sheer bliss when I shut the last lunch-box and had the house to myself. Then I spent an uninterrupted morning writing, which I love. When the kids came home, I enjoyed their noise after the quiet of the day.

Later, peace **descended** again, and my husband and I enjoyed another pleasure—intimacy. Sometimes just the knowledge that he wants me can bring me joy.

You never know where happiness will turn up next. When I asked friends what made them happy, some mentioned seemingly insignificant moments. "I hate shopping," one friend said. "but there's a clerk who always chats and really cheers me up." Another friend loves the telephone "Every time it rings, I know someone is thinking about me."

I get a thrill from driving. One day I stopped to let a school bus turn onto a side road. The driver grinned and gave me the thumbs up sign. We were two **allies** in a world of mad motorists. It made me smile.

We all experience moments like these. Too few of us register them as happiness.

Psychologists tell us that to be happy we need a blend of enjoyable leisure time and satisfying work. I doubt that my great-grandmother, who raised 14 children and took in washing, had much of either. *She did have a network of close friends and family, and maybe this was what fulfilled her*. If she was happy with what she had, perhaps it was because she didn't expect life to be very different.

We, on the other hand, with so many choices and such pressure to succeed in every area, have turned happiness into one more thing we "gotta have." We're so self-conscious about our "right" to it that it's making us miserable. So we chase it and equate it with wealth and success, without noticing that the people who have those things aren't necessarily happier.

While happiness may be more complex for us, the solution is the same as ever. Happiness isn't about what happens to us — it's about how we perceive what happens to us. It's the knack of finding a positive for every negative, and viewing a setback as a challenge. It's not wishing for what we don't have, but enjoying what we do possess.

我们四处追逐幸福，而幸福其实就在我们身边。

一天。我问哥哥伊恩："你感到幸福吗？"他回答说："可以说幸福，也可以说不幸福，这要看你指什么了。"

"那你告诉我，"我说，"最近一次你感到幸福是什么时候？"

"1967 年 4 月，"他答道。

我真不该对一个游戏生活的人提出这么严肃的问题。但伊恩的回答却给了我一个启示：我们想到的幸福时刻通常是一些非同寻常的事，一种纯粹的快乐——但是随着年龄的增长，这种快乐好像越来越少了。

对一个孩子来说，幸福有着梦幻般的色彩。记得我曾在新鲜的干草丛中捉迷藏；在树林里玩"警察与小偷"；在学校的戏剧里扮演有台词的角色。当然，孩子也有情绪低落的时候。但是，因为赢得一场比赛，或得了一辆新单车，他们会毫不掩饰地快乐到极点。

到了青少年时期，幸福观逐渐转变。突然间，幸福就建立在激动、爱情、名气甚至是脸上的青春痘能否在晚会前消失这样的事上。我清楚地记得大家都去参加一个舞会，而我未被邀请时的痛苦。但也记得，在另一次活动中，我意外地与一个貌似约翰·特拉沃尔塔的人共舞时的兴奋。

成年后，心灵深处最令人喜悦的是生育、爱情和婚姻。所有这些同时也带来了责任和丧失。爱情可能会消逝。性爱也不总是如意，心爱的人可能会死去。对于成人来说，幸福很复杂。

字典里幸福的定义是"幸运"或"好运"，但我认为幸福更好的定义是"感受快乐的能力"。更多地享受我们拥有的一切，我们就能更多地享受幸福。但是，爱与被爱，友人相伴，简单的生活，甚至健康的体魄，这些细碎的快乐却很容易被我们忽视。

我合计了一下昨日的幸福时光，首先我准备好了最后一个午餐饭盒，独享整个房间，感受无比的幸福。然后，整个早上，我都在写作而无人打扰，这是我乐于做的。孩子们回到家，我又享受着寂静一天后的热闹。

不久，再次恢复宁静，我和丈夫享受另一种快乐——亲热。有时候只要想到他需要我，就能给我带来快乐。

你永远不会知道幸福下一次会在什么时候出现。当我问起朋友，什么能给他们带来幸福时，有些人会提到一些看似微不足道的小事。"我讨厌购物，"一个朋友说，"但有一个健谈的售货员的确令我很开心。"另一个朋友喜欢接电话，"每次电话一响，我就知道有人想我了。"

我喜欢开车的刺激。一天，我停下来，让一辆学校班车拐到路边。那个司机咧嘴一笑，会意地竖起大拇指。在一个充满飙车党的世界，我们俩结成了同盟。这让我很开心。

我们都有过类似的经历。但很少有人能意识到这就是幸福。

心理学家告诉我们，幸福既需要愉快的休闲时间，也需要满意的工作。我的曾祖母让我很疑惑，她养育了 14 个孩子，还要给别人洗衣服，看起来，她并没有休闲的时间，也没有满意的工作。但她有几个亲密的朋友和和睦的家。或许，这已使她很满足了。如果说她因自己拥有的一切感到幸福，或许是因为她并不希望生活是另一番样子。

另一方面，我们因为有太多的选择及想在各个领域成功的压力，让我们把幸福变成"必须得到"的一种东西。我们自私地以为我们有"权"得到它，这也是我们痛苦的根源。所以我们去追求幸福，并将它同财富和成功联系起来，而没有意识到拥有财富和成功的人并不一定更幸福。

对我们来说，幸福是复杂多样的，但获得幸福的方式却是相同的。幸福不是发生在我们周围的事——而是我们如何去看待周围发生的事。这是变不利为有利，化挫折为激励的秘诀。幸福并非是乞求我们未得到的，而是享受我们此刻所拥有的一切。

核心单词

extraordinary [iks'trɔːdnri] *adj.* 异常的；特别的，非凡的

pinnacle ['pinəkl]　*n.* 尖顶；山顶，山峰

sheer [ʃiə]　*adj.* 全然的；纯粹的

unreserved ['ʌnri'zəːvd] *adj.* 不隐瞒的；坦率的；完全的

descend [di'send]　*v.* 下来，下降

allies [ə'laɪz]　*n.* 协约国；同盟国

实用句型

She did have a network of close friends and family, and maybe this was what fulfilled her.

她有几个亲密的朋友和和睦的家庭，或许，这已使她很满足了。

① did 在这里起强调作用，可翻译为"确实"。

② a network of 一些，类似的表达还有 a crowd of 许多；a number of 一些等固定搭配。

翻译行不行

1. 在精力充沛的年轻时代，他从未停止对自己梦想的追求。(chase after)

....

2. 他把座位让给了一位老人。(give up)

....

3. 塞翁失马，安知非福；塞翁得马，安知非祸。(on the other hand)

....

Five Balls of Life
生命中的五个球

· Meade ·

In a university **commencement** address several years ago, Brian Dyson, CEO of Coca Cola Enterprises, spoke of the relation of work to one's other commitments:

Imagine life as a game in which you are juggling some five balls in the air. You name them work, family, health, friends and spirit and you're keeping all of these in the air. You will soon understand that work is a rubber ball. If you drop it, it will **bounce** back.

But the other four balls family, health, friends and spirit are made of glass. If you drop one of these, they will be irrevocably **scuffed**, marked, nicked, damaged or even shattered. They will never be the same. You must understand that and strive for balance in your life. How?

Don't undermine your worth by comparing yourself with others. It is because we are different and each of us is special.

Don't set your goals by what other people deem important. Only you know what is best for you.

Don't take for granted the things closest to your heart. Cling to them as they would be your life, for without them, life is meaningless.

Don't let your life slip through your fingers by living in the past or for the future. By living your life one day at a time, you live ALL the days of your life.

Don't give up when you still have something to give. Nothing is really over until the moment you stop trying.

Don't be afraid to admit that you are less than perfect. It is this **fragile** thread that binds us to each together.

Don't be afraid to **encounter** risks. It is by taking chances that we learn how to be brave.

Don't shut love out of your life by saying it's impossible to find. The quickest way to receive love is to give it ; the fastest way to lose love is to hold it too tightly ; and the best way to keep love is to give it wings.

Don't run through life so fast that you forget not only where you've been, but also where you are going.

Don't forget, a person's greatest emotional need is to feel appreciated.

Don't be afraid to learn. Knowledge is weightless, a treasure you can always carry easily.

Don't use time or words carelessly. Neither can be retrieved.

Life is not a race, but a journey to be **savored** each step of the way.

Yesterday is history, tomorrow is a mystery and today is a gift: that's why we call it "The Present".

几年前，在一所大学的开学典礼上，可口可乐的首席执行官布赖恩·戴森讲到工作与其他义务的关系：

想象生命是一场不停丢掷五个球于空中的游戏。这五个球分别是工作、家庭、健康、朋友和心灵，而且你很努力地掷着这五个球，不让它们落地。很快你就会了解工作是一个橡皮球。如果你不幸失手落下它，它还是会弹回来的。

但是家庭、健康、朋友和心灵这四个球是用玻璃做成的。一旦你失手落下，它们可能会少了一角，留下无法挽回的记号、刻痕、损坏甚至碎落一地。它们将无法再像以前那样。你必须了解这个道理，并且为平衡你的生命而努力。但要怎样才能做到呢？

别拿自己和他人比较，这只会降低你的价值。因为我们都是独一无二的，因为我们每一个人都很特别。

别人认为重要的事不一定是你的目标。只有你自己知道什么是最适合你的。

不要将贴近你的心的人、事物视为理所当然。你必须将他们视为生命一般，认真对待。因为没有他们，生命将失去意义。

别让你的生命总是在依恋过去的种种或是在未来的寄望中逝去。如果你活在每个当下，那就活好你生命中的每一天。

当你还能给予的时候别轻言放弃。只要你不放弃，就有无限延伸的可能。

别害怕承认你并不完美。正因如此，我们才得以藉由这脆弱的细丝紧密地串绑在一起。

遇到危险时别害怕。正因如此，我们才得以藉由这些机会学习勇敢。

别以爱太难寻找作为借口而紧闭你的心扉。最迅速找到爱的方法就是给予你的爱；最快速失去爱的方法就是紧紧地守着你的爱不放；维持爱的最好方式就是给爱一双翅膀。

不要匆忙地度过你的一生，那匆忙让你忘了曾经到过哪里，也让你忘了你要去哪里。

别忘记，人类情感上最大的需要是感恩。

不要害怕学习。知识没有重量，它是可以随身携带的珍宝。

别漫不经心地蹉跎光阴或口无遮拦。时间与言词两者都是一放就收不回来的。

生命不是一场赛跑，而是一步一个脚印的旅程。

昨天已是历史，明天还是未知，而今天则是上天赐予的礼物：那就是我们为什么称它为"现在"（Present）的原因。

Practising
& Exercise

核心单词

commencement [kə'mensmənt] *n.* 学位授予典礼；毕业典礼

bunce [bʌntʃ] *v.* 弹起，弹回；跃，蹦蹦跳跳

scuff [skʌf] *v.* 拖着脚走路；使磨损

fragile ['frædʒail] *adj.* 易碎的；易损坏的；脆弱的；虚弱的

encounter [in'kauntə] *v.* 遇到（困难，危险等）；意外地遇见

savor ['seivə] *n.* 滋味；气味；风趣，趣味

实用句型

Imagine life as a game in which you are juggling some five balls in the air.

想象生命是一场不停丢掷 5 个球于空中的游戏。

①这里是"in+which"引导的限定性定语从句，修饰限定 a game，介词后的关系词不能省。

② as a game 像个游戏，类似的表达还有 as a brid 像只鸟。另有 as long as 只要，as far as 尽……就…… 等固定搭配。

翻译行不行

1. 宴会的日期尚未确定。(in the air)

....

2. 鱼缸是玻璃做的。(be made of)

....

3. 我的英语比她的英语要差好多。(compare with)

....

The Paradox of Happiness
矛盾幸福感

· Timothy ·

What is the definition of "happiness"?Is it material wealth filled with fancy cars, a dream house, **extravagant** furs and jewelry? Or is happiness simply having a roof over your head? Food in the fridge? Having a child? A pet? A swimming pool? A designer Gucci bag? Parents? Grandchildren? Love? Money? The perfect job? Winning the Lottery?

According to the *American Heritage Dictionary*, "happiness" is derived from the Middle English word hap—meaning "Luck." But does happiness really have anything to do with "luck?" Based on this description, one could assume that if you avoided a fatal traffic accident but got fired by coming late to work, you would be filled with "happiness?" Is it luck or what you make of it? Maybe, "happiness" is exactly defined by its indirect alias: happiness—perhaps, happiness is in fact defined by the fortune that we permit to happen.

Do you recall a time—let's say when you were about 5 years old—what defined happiness back then? Was it getting a puppy for Christmas? Or maybe, you were a child of divorce ;

and all you wanted was for Mom and Dad to get back together again? Then as you got older, you were hoping that someone would ask you to the prom that would've made your day, maybe your life for the moment. During college, good grades made you happy, but it was short-lived. *Because in the real world, you had to look for a job, and competition was stark.* It's an employer's world you thought. But then, you got the perfect job—now you could be happy—or could you?

Life requires more than just what we want. **Inevitably**, one must understand to truly find "happiness," he must make his own happiness "happen". Sounds a bit **redundant**, but truthfully, there is no set guidelines that will bring one happiness. There is no "magic wand" we can wave to bring joy into our lives. Human nature thrives on the thrill of the chase. We dream and we hope for the next big break—it is the grand adventure of living.

We are hopeless creatures of comfort. We like having and accumulating things. Whether one admits to it or not, to a certain degree, we all try to keep up with "the Jones". We work so we can pay our rents, **mortgages**, credit card debts, school loans, car payments... the list goes on and on. And at some point, we realize, that aside from having most of what we want, we still aren't happy. Now since we've learned to adapt to new standards which we've created for ourselves, we find that we have less time, less patience, less sleep, which equates to more stress, more worry and more aggravation. So, is happiness honestly just comprised of "things"?

Sometimes, we **virtually** trade our lives for not only basic necessities, but for excessive items and services as well. We become so obsessed with finding happiness, that we lose sight of the fact that happiness is within—always. Certainly you've heard of individuals trying to "find themselves", or "rediscover themselves". The reason they are attempting these innovative approaches is because they are seeking inner happiness. But the point has been missed: Happiness is already there.

Disappointments and tragedies in life will come and go, but happiness never leaves you. The human's capacity to be resilient to trials is unfathomable. We can lose our jobs, but be grateful for our spouses. We can lose our homes to nature, but be thankful to be alive.

Happiness is a perception of each individual. We are instinctively compelled to find fault in our lives. By human nature, we begin our "fault-finding" mission the moment we're capable of free-thinking. It is then, that we lose sense of self-worth and the bigger picture of vitality altogether. Stuck in the patterns of the happiness paradox, we simply cannot find where our happiness has gone.

It's not a matter of bargaining, it's not an issue of money or fame— instead, happiness is what you resolve to accept. If we live through **optimistic** hope ; if we dare to dream ; if we empower ourselves to fully live ; then we have regained our sense of happiness. There is no in between. There is no other replacement. We only have one physical life to live— we have no choice but to make the most of it.

蒂莫西

"幸福"是什么？幸福是拥有豪华的汽车、理想的居室、名贵的裘皮和珠宝等物质上的富足吗？或者，简单的只是有个遮风避雨的住所，冰箱里有食物，有孩子、宠物、游泳池、个性的包，有父母、子孙、有爱情、金钱和理想的工作，彩票中奖了呢？

在《美国传统字典》中，幸福是从中古英语"Hap"一词演变而来的。"Hap"意为"好运"。但是，幸福真的与"好运"有关联吗？基于此，想想看，如果你在一场必死无疑的交通事故中幸免于难，却因此迟到，导致被老板炒鱿鱼。对此，你会感到"幸福"吗？这是好运吗？还是要看个人如何看待这个问题呢？或许，确切地说，幸福的定义应当直接从它的词源来看——事实上，幸福或许就是命中注定要发生的事情。

你能回忆起你5岁时对幸福的理解吗？那时，幸福是从圣诞树上摘下的一只小狗吗？或者爸爸妈妈离婚了，你唯一的愿望就是他们能和好如初，重新生活在一起？当你渐渐长大，你希望有人会邀请你参加舞会，希望所有的日子都凝固在那一天、那一刻。上大学期间，考试得了高分让你无比开心，但这种幸福感都是短暂的。因为在现实中，你得找一份工作，而社会竞争也相当激烈。于是，你就会想，这是一个雇主的世界。随后，你找到了一份理想的工作——现在的你很开心，是吗？

生活向我们索要的远比我们想要的多。一个人必须明白，要想真正找到幸福，他就必须让自己幸福。可能听起来有些多余，但确是如此——生活中，没有能带来幸福的现成指南，也没有挥一挥就能带来欢乐的魔棒。人性在追求幸福的刺激中不断升级、完善。我们梦想着、期望着下一个大的转变——这就是生活中的大冒险了。

我们是无助的享乐者，喜欢拥有和积攒东西。不论人们承认与否，一定程度上，我们都在相互攀比。我们之所以工作，是因为要付房租，偿还抵押贷款，还清信用卡透支费用，偿付助学贷款，买车，等。此类费用接连而至，让我们应接不暇。于是，我们会突然意识到，尽管拥有了想要的一切，我们仍然不幸福。自从适应了自己定下的新生活标准，我们的时间短了，耐性没了，睡眠少了，但压力大了，焦虑多了，脾气也暴躁了。鉴于此，幸福真的是由"物质"组成的吗？

事实上，有时，我们不仅用生命交换生活必需品，还用生命交换多余的物质享受和服务。我们这般沉迷于追求幸福，却忽略了一个事实——幸福一直就在我们心中。当然，你一定听过这样的事，即有些人一直都在苦苦"找寻自我"或"重新发现自我"。他们创新尝试的理由只不过是想找寻心灵深处的幸福。但他们忽略了一点，即幸福从头至尾都在心中。

失望和悲伤在生命中交替轮回，但幸福从不会舍你而去。人类对困难的适应能力无可限量。我们可以失去工作，但会为拥有爱人而感恩不已；我们可以流离失所，但会为活着而心存感激。

幸福是个人的一种感知。我们本能地受限于外界，找寻着生活的瑕疵。出于人的天性，我们从有能力自由思考的那刻起，就开始对生活吹毛求疵。也就在那时，我们失去了对自我价值的认知，也失去了生命的活力，陷入幸福的矛盾中，找不到幸福的方向。

幸福是你决定去接受的东西，没有任何商量的余地，它与金钱或名誉毫无瓜葛。只要我们活在乐观希望之中。敢于大胆梦想，活得简单纯粹，那么，我们就会重新拥有幸福的感觉。那种感觉并非悬于幸与不幸之间的真空地带，也无任何替代品。我们只能活一次——除了好好活着，我们别无选择。

Practising
& Exercise

核心单词

paradox ['pærədɔks]　*n.* 自相矛盾的议论

extravagant [iks'trævəgənt]　*adj.* 奢侈的；浪费的；过分的

inevitably [in'evitəbli]　*adv.* 不可避免地；必然地

redundant [ri'dʌndənt]　*adj.* 多余的，过剩的

mortgage ['mɔːgidʒ]　*n.* 抵押；抵押借款

virtually ['vɜːtjuəli]　*adv.* 实际上，事实上，差不多

optimistic [ˌɔpti'mistik]　*adj.* 乐观的

实用句型

Because in the real world, you had to look for a job, and competition was stark. 因为在现实中，你必须找一份工作，而且社会竞争也相当激烈。

①这里是由 because 引导的原因状语从句。

② look for 寻找，类似的表达还有 look up 查找；look after 照顾；look at 看等固定搭配。

翻译行不行

1. 他们按年龄分成了三组。(according to)

......

2. 实际上，我是想和你一起去的。(in fact)

......

3. 她退休后一直同一些朋友保持着联系。(keep up with)

......

Enthusiasm Takes You Further
热情带你前进

• Anonymous •

Years ago, when I started looking for my first job, wise advisers urged, "Barbara, be enthusiastic! **Enthusiasm** will take you further than any amount of experience. "

How right they were. Enthusiastic people can turn a boring drive into an adventure, extra work into opportunity and strangers into friends.

"Nothing great was ever achieved without enthusiasm. " wrote Ralph Waldo Emerson. It is the paste that helps you hang in there when the going gets tough. It is the inner voice that whispers, 'I can do it !" when others shout, 'No, you can't."

It took years and years for the early work of Barbara Mc—Clintock, a geneticist who won the 1983 Nobel Prize in medicine, to be generally accepted. Yet she didn't let up on her experiments. Work was such a deep pleasure for her that she never thought of stopping.

We are all born with wide—eyed, enthusiastic wonder as anyone knows who has ever seen an infant's delight at the jingle of keys or the scurrying of a beetle.

It is this childlike wonder that gives enthusiastic people such a youthful air, whatever their age.

At 90, cellist Pablo Casals would start his day by playing Bach. As the music flowed through his fingers, his stooped shoulders would straighten and joy would reappear in his eyes. Music, for Casals, was an elixir that made life a never ending adventure. As author and poet Samuel Ullman once wrote, "Years wrinkle the skin, but to give up enthusiasm wrinkles the soul."

How do you rediscover the enthusiasm of your childhood? The answer, I believe, lies in the word itself. "Enthusiasm" comes from the Greek and means "God within". And what is God within is but an abiding sense of love—proper love of self (self-acceptance) and, from that, love of others.

Enthusiastic people also love what they do, regardless of money or title or power. If we cannot do what we love as a full-time career, we can do it as a part-time avocation, like the head of a state who paints, the nun who runs marathons, the executive who handcrafts furniture.

Elizabeth Layton of Wellsville, Kan, was 68 before she began to draw. This activity ended bouts of depression that had **plagued** her for at least 30 years, and the quality of her work led one critic to say, "I am **tempted** to call Layton a **genius**." Elizabeth has rediscovered her enthusiasm.

We can't afford to waste tears on "might-have-beens". We need to turn the tears into sweat as we go after "what-can-be".

We need to live each moment **wholeheartedly**, with all our senses—finding pleasure in the fragrance of a back-yard garden, the **crayoned** picture of a six-year-old, the **enchanting** beauty of a rainbow. It is such enthusiastic love of life that puts a sparkle in our eyes, a lilt in our steps and smooths the wrinkles from our souls.

佚 名

多年前，我开始寻求第一份工作。聪慧的辅导员们催促说："芭芭拉，热情点！热情会比任何经验让你走得更远。"

他们说得真对啊！热情的人能让一次枯燥的旅行变成冒险，超额的工作变成机会，陌生人变成朋友。

"没有热情，什么大事也干不了。"拉尔夫·沃尔德·埃莫森这样写道。它像浆糊把你粘在那里，当困难沉重时你仍能坚持。当别人冲你喊着："不行，你不行"时，它是内心的低语："我能行！"

1983 年诺贝尔医学奖获得者，遗传学家芭芭拉·麦克林多克的早期研究工作在很多年后才被广泛认可，但是她并没有停止实验工作。工作本身给她带来许多乐趣，她从未想过要停止。

我们天生好奇，充满热望，你看新出生的婴儿对钥匙的叮铃作响和疾驶而过的甲壳虫总是兴致勃勃。

是这般孩童似的好奇给了热情的人这般年轻生动的气韵，

不管他们的实际有多老。

　　90 岁高龄的大提琴演奏家帕布罗·卡萨尔仍然以演奏巴赫的曲子作为一天的序曲。当音乐从指间流出，他佝偻的肩膀便会舒展，喜悦重新浮现在他的双眼里。音乐对于卡萨尔来说不亚于仙丹，使他的人生变成一场永不停息的历险。正如作家、诗人萨缨尔·乌尔曼曾经写道："时间令皮肤起皱，放弃热情则令灵魂起皱。"

　　你该如何重获儿时的热情？我相信，答案在这个词身上。"热情"来自于希腊语"内心的神"，内心的神就是坚持不懈的爱，适当地爱自己即自我接纳，然后衍生出来爱别人。

　　热情的人也会爱他们从事的工作，不管金钱、名气或权力。如果我们不能全职做自己热爱的事情，也可以兼职做呀，就像画画的州长，跑马拉松的修女和做家具的行政长官。

　　住在堪萨斯州威尔士维尔市的伊丽莎白·莱顿，68 岁时开始画画，这一举动令烦扰了她至少 30 年的抑郁症不治而愈，而且她的作品令一个评论家说："我忍不住要管莱顿叫天才。"伊丽莎白重获了她的热情。

　　我们浪费不起眼泪在"如果当初那样该多好"之类的想法上。我们应该将眼泪化为汗水，辛勤追赶"将会怎样"的梦想。

　　我们需要每分每秒都全身心地生活，用全副感官去感觉：后院花园的花香，六岁孩童的蜡笔画，美丽彩虹的魔力。对生活的热情和爱让我们的眼眸熠熠闪光，令我们的步履轻盈并抚平我们灵魂上的皱纹。

Practising & Exercise 实战提升篇

核心单词

urge [ə:dʒ] v. 激励；怂恿极力主张；强烈要求

enthusiasm [in'θju:ziæzəm] n. 热心，热情，热忱

plague [pleig] v. 使苦恼；烦忧；折磨

tempt [tempt] v. 引诱，诱惑，勾引；吸引，引起

genius ['dʒi:njəs] n. 天资，天赋，天才，英才

wholeheartedly [həul'ha:tidli] adv. 全心全意地；全神贯注地

crayon ['kreiən] n. 蜡笔；炭笔

enchanting [in'tʃɑ:ntiŋ] adj. 迷人的，使人着魔的

实用句型

It is this childlike wonder that gives enthusiastic people such a youthful air, whatever their age. 是这种孩童似的好奇给了热情的人这般年轻生动的气韵，不管他们实际有多老。

①这里是 it is...that 的强调句结构。

② whatever 不管，诸如此类，类似的表达还有 whoever 无论谁；whichever 无论哪一个等。

翻译行不行

1. 他的成功缘于他的努力。(lie in)

......

2. 他不顾危险地爬上了高塔。(regardless of)

......

3. 完成这项任务至少需要两天的时间。(at least)

......

Today I Will be Master of My Emotions
做自己情绪的主人

· Warren ·

The tides advance ; the tides recede. Winter goes and summer comes. Summer wanes and the cold increases. The sun rises ; the sun sets. The moon is full ; the moon is black. The birds arrive! the birds depart. Flowers bloom ; flowers fade. Seeds are sown ; harvests are **reaped**. All nature is a circle of moods and I am a part of nature and so, like the tides, my moods will rise ; my moods will fall.

It is one of nature's tricks, little understood, that each day I awaken with moods that have changed from yesterday. Yesterday's joy will become today's sadness ; yet today's sadness will grow into tomorrow's joy. Inside me is a wheel, constantly turning from sadness to joy, from **exultation** to depression, from happiness to **melancholy**. Like the flowers, today's full bloom of joy will fade and withers into despondency, yet I will remember that as today's dead flower carries the seed of tomorrow's bloom so, too, does today's sadness carry the seed of tomorrow's joy.

And how will I master these emotions so that each day will

be productive? For unless my mood is right the day will be a failure. Trees and plants depend on the weather to flourish but I make my own weather, yea I transport it with me.

And how will I master my emotions so that every day is a happy day, and a productive one? I will learn this secret of the ages: Weak is he who **permits** his thoughts to control his actions ; strong is he who forces his actions to control his thoughts. Each day, when I awaken, I will follow this plan of battle before I am **captured** by the forces of sadness, self-pity and failure—

If I feel depressed I will sing.

If I feel sad I will laugh.

If I feel ill I will double my labor.

If I feel fear I will plunge ahead.

If I feel inferior I will wear new garments.

If I feel uncertain I will raise my voice.

If I feel poverty I will think of wealth to come.

If I feel incompetent I will remember past success.

If I feel insignificant I will remember my goals.

Henceforth, I will know that only those with inferior ability can always be at their best, and I am not inferior. There will be days when I must constantly struggle against forces which would tear me down. Those such as despair and sadness are simple to recognize but there are others which approach with a smile and the hand of friendship and they can also **destroy** me. Against them, too, I must never **relinquish** control—

If I become overconfident I will recall my failures.

If I overindulge I will think of past hungers.

If I feel complacency I will remember my competition.

If I enjoy moments of greatness I will remember moments of shame.

If I feel all-powerful I will try to stop the wind.

If I attain great wealth I will remember one unfed mouth.

If I become overly proud I will remember a moment of weakness.

If I feel my skill is unmatched I will look at the stars.

Henceforth I will recognize and identify the mystery of moods in all mankind, and in me. From this moment I am prepared to control whatever personality awakes in me each day. I will master my moods through positive action and when I master my moods I will control my destiny. I will become master of myself. I will become great.

沃 伦

潮涨潮落；冬去夏来；暑消寒长，日升日落；月圆月缺，雁来雁往；花开花谢，春种秋收。自然界万事万物都处于情绪的循环变化中，而我也是大自然的一部分，所以，我也有如潮水般的情绪，时涨时落。

很少有人懂得，这是大自然的一种愚弄。每天早晨，当我醒来时，心情都与昨天有所不同。昨天的欢乐可能成了今天的悲伤，然而，今天的悲伤可能成为明天的欢乐。在我的内心深处，好像有一个轮子，不断地从悲伤转到欢乐，从狂喜转到绝望。从快乐变为忧郁。就像花儿，今天绽放的喜悦会慢慢消退，变成明天凋谢的绝望，但是我会记住，今天枯萎的花朵同样孕育着明天绽放的种子，正如今天的悲伤也播种了明天的欢乐。

要让每一天都卓有成效，我该怎样控制这些情绪呢？如果我心浮气躁，那么这一天将会在失败中度过。植物树木的繁盛依赖于天气，但我创造着自己的天气，可以随时掌控。

那么我要怎样控制自己的情绪，让每一天都充满快乐和成效呢？我要学会这个千古秘诀：行为受控于情绪的人是弱者，强者只会用行为控制情绪。每天醒来时，我要这样对抗悲伤、自怜、失败的情绪，这样才不会被它们俘虏——

如果我觉得沮丧，就放声歌唱。

如果我感到悲伤，就露出微笑。

如果我身体不适，就加倍工作。

如果我陷入恐惧，就埋头苦干。

如果我自惭形秽，就换上新装。

如果我犹疑不决，就提高分贝。

如果我囊中羞涩，就想象财富将至。

如果我力不从心，就回忆以往的成功。

如果我自轻自贱，就铭记自己的目标。

从今以后，我懂得，只有能力较低的人才会一直处于最佳状态，而我并非低能者。总有些时候，有些力量企图将我毁灭，而我必须不断地与之对抗。其中失望与悲伤很容易识破，但是，还有其他一些力量往往带着微笑靠近我，并向我伸出友谊之手，而它们同样也能将我毁灭。我同样要与它们抗争，永远不放弃对它们的掌控——

如果我骄傲自负，就追寻失败的记忆。

如果我沉湎享乐，就想想挨饿的过去。

如果我安于现状，就想想竞争对手。

如果我居功自傲，就回想屈辱之时。

如果我自以为是，就试着让风儿止步。

如果我腰缠万贯，想想那些食不果腹的人。

如果我目空一切，就想起自己怯懦的时候。

如果我不可一世，就抬起头来仰望群星。

从此，我能识别和辨认人类所有情绪变化的奥秘，包括自己的内在。从今以后，无论我的个人情绪如何变化，我都会随时做出积极的行动来控制。一旦我控制了自己的情绪，就掌握了自己的命运，也将成为自己的主人，变得卓尔不群。

Practising

实战 提升篇

& Exercise

核心单词

reap [ri:p] *v.* 收获；获得，得到

exultation [ˌegzʌl'teiʃən] *n.* 狂喜；洋洋得意

melancholy ['melənkəli] *n.* 忧郁；愁思

permit [pə(:)'mit] *v.* 允许，许可，准许

capture ['kæptʃə] *v.* 捕获；俘虏占领，*n.* 俘获，获得

destroy [dis'trɔi] *v.* 毁坏，破坏

relinquish [ri'liŋkwiʃ] *v.* 放弃；撤出；交出，让与

实用句型

If I feel poverty I will think of wealth to come.

如果我囊中羞涩，就想象财富将至。

① if 在这里是"如果"的意思，引导一个真实条件句。

② think of 想到，考虑，类似的表达还有 think about 考虑；think over 仔细考虑等固定搭配。

翻译行不行

1. 微言起风波。（grow into）

....

2. 他的一家人全靠他养活。（depend on）

....

3. 经过讨论，他们准备写一篇文章来提出自己的看法。（prepare to）

....

Seven Secrets to a Great Life
非凡人生的七大秘诀

• Anonymous •

A great life doesn't happen by accident. A great life is the result of **allocating** your time, energy, thoughts, and hard work towards what you want your life to be. Stop setting yourself up for stress and failure, and start setting up your life to support success and ease. A great life is the result of using the 24/7 you get in a creative and thoughtful way, instead of just what comes next. Customize these "secrets" to fit your own needs and style, and start creating your own great life today!

1. S—Simplify. A great life is the result of simplifying your life. People often misinterpret what simplify means. It's not a way to remove work from your life. When you focus on simplifying your life, you free up energy and time for the work that you enjoy and the purpose for which you are here. *In order to create a great life, you will have to make room for it in yours first.*

2. E—Effort. A great life is the result of your best effort. Creating a great life requires that you make some adjustments. It may mean reevaluating how you spend your time, or choosing to spend your money in a different way. It may mean looking for new ways to spend your energy that **coincide** with your particular definition of a great life. Life will reward your best effort.

3. C—Create **Priorities**. A great life is the result of creating priorities. It's easy to spend your days just responding to the next thing that gets your attention, instead of intentionally using the time, energy and money you have in a way that's important to you. Focus on removing the **obstacles** that get in the way of you making sure you are honoring your priorities.

4. R—Reserves. A great life is the result of having reserves—reserves of things, time, space, energy, money. With reserves, you acquire far more than you need—not 6 months living expenses, but 5 years worth ; not 15 minutes of free time, 1 day. Reserves are important because they reduce the fear of consequences, and that allows you to make decisions based on what you really want instead of what the fear decides for you.

5. E—**Eliminate** distractions. A great life is the result of eliminating distractions. Up to 75% of your **mental** energy can be tied up in things that are draining and distracting you. Eliminating distractions can be a difficult concept to many people, since they haven't really considered that there is another way to live. Look around at someone's life you admire. What do they do that you would like to **incorporate** into your own life? Ask them how they did it. Find ways to free up your mental energy for things that are more important to you.

6. T—Thoughts. A great life is the result of controlling your thoughts so that you accept and allow for the possibility that it actually can happen to you! Your belief in the outcome will directly dictate how successful you are. Motivated people have specific goals and look for ways to achieve them. Believing there is a solution to the same old problems you encounter year after year is

vitally important to creating a life that you love.

7. S—Start. A great life is the result of starting. There's the old saying everyone's familiar with "a journey of a thousand miles begins with a single step." In order to even move from the couch to the refrigerator, you have to start. There's no better time to start than today. Don't wait for a raise, or until the kids get older, or the weather is better. Today, right now, is the right day to start to take a step in the direction of your heart's desires. It's what you do TODAY that will make a difference in your life tomorrow.

佚　名

非凡的人生不是偶然产生的。它需要合理分配自己的时间、精力、心思并为实现自己的生活目标而努力。走出忧虑和失败、全身心地迎接成功和安逸。非凡人生是利用分分秒秒来创造和思索的结果而不是坐等。让我们从今天开始，根据下面的"秘诀"和自身情况，创建属于自己的非凡人生吧！

1．化繁为简。非凡的人生源于简化你的生活。人们往往误解了简化的含义，即不参加工作。当生活真正简化，你就会有时间和精力从事喜欢的工作，并为之奋斗。创建非凡的人生，首先要有自己的空间。

2．不懈努力。非凡的人生源于个人的艰苦努力。它需要对你的生活做些调整，它可能需要你重新分配时间，或调整理财方式；它可能要你寻求新的方法以使你将精力放在你自己所定义的非凡人生上。有付出就会有回报。

3. 分清主次。非凡的人生源于分清主次。人很容易被琐碎的事所吸引，而不能将时间、精力、金钱放在重要的事上，要集中精力先清除在自己首要解决问题上的绊脚石。

4. 有备无患。非凡的人生源于懂得储备——储备物品、时间、空间、精力和金钱。有了这些储备，你的获得就会远远多于所期望的——你得到的会是五年的生活费，而不是六个月的；你得到的会是一整天的闲暇时间，而不只是 15 分钟。储备很重要，因为它能减少你的顾虑，还会使你依自己的目标来做决定而不是被顾虑所支配。

5. 专心致志。非凡的人生源于专注。做事三心二意，会耗费一个人 75% 以上的精力。很多人不知道如何清除杂念，因为他们从未想过换种方式生活。看看周围那些令你羡慕的人的生活吧。看自己能从他们身上学到些什么？向他们请教，寻求专注的方式，把精力集中到真正重要的事情上。

6. 坚定信念。非凡的人生源于控制你的信念。信念会令事情真的发生，也会直接告诉你，你是多么的成功。有动力的人目标明确，并会想尽一切办法去实现。生活中会反复遇到很多问题，相信这些问题终会解决，是创造美好生活的关键。

7. 立刻行动。非凡人生源于行动。有句大家熟悉的古谚，"千里之行始于足下"。即使是想从沙发走到冰箱前，也需要亲自行动。从今天开始行动吧，不要再找借口，说等涨工资了，等孩子长大了，或者等天气好了再说吧。从今天开始，去努力实现心中的梦想，这是最好的时机。只有从今天就开始，你的明天才会更好。

Practising

& Exercise 实战 提升篇

核心单词

allocate ['æləukeit] v. 分派；分配

coincide [,kəuin'said] v. 同时发生；相符，巧合

priority [prai'ɔriti] n. 优先，重点；优先权

obstacle ['ɔbstəkl] n. 障碍（物）；妨碍

eliminate [i'limineit] v. 排除，消除，消灭

mental ['mentl] adj. 精神的，心理的；智力的

incorporate [in'kɔ:pəreit] v. 包含，吸收，使并入

实用句型

In order to creat a great life，you will have to make room for it in yours first.

创建非凡的人生，首先要有自己的空间。

①这里是 in order to 引导的目的状语从句。

② make room for 给……腾出空间，类似的表达还有 leave room for 为……留出空间；take up room 占有空间等固定搭配。

翻译行不行

1. 这个办法是他偶然想到的。(by accident)

....

2. 真没想到，考试的结果这么好。(the result of)

....

3. 他不仅没有帮我们，反而还嘲笑我们。(instead of)

....

A-B-C Method of Managing Attitudes
处事方法 A–B–C

• Anonymous •

As an airport **skycap** checked through a customer at curb-side, he accidentally knocked over the man's luggage. He quickly collected the fallen bags and apologized for the **mishap**. *Unappeased, the traveler burst into an angry tirade, raging and swearing at the skycap for his clumsiness.* Throughout the traveler's rant, the baggage handler simply apologized and smiled. The angry man continued berating the skycap, until he finally headed off to catch his plane. Even then the baggage handler remained calm and passively smiled.

The next customer in line witnessed the incident and marveled at the skycap's professionalism and control. "I have never seen such **restraint** and humility." he said. "How do you keep your cool when somebody is attacking you so **viciously**?"

"It's easy." the skycap answered. "He's going to Denver, but his bags are going to Detroit."

That is certainly ONE way of managing attitudes, but here is a more constructive approach.

Have you heard of the A–B–C method of managing your

attitude? It's simple and effective.

"A" stands for the "Activating Event". Let's say you get stuck in traffic. The traffic jam is the activating event.

"B" stands for your "Belief System". You believe that traffic is only getting worse and you'll have more and more days like this ahead.

"C" stands for the "Consequence of the Event". You become angry. You want to honk your horn. Your stomach is tied in knots and you bang the dashboard with your fist.

The problem is... most people jump directly from "A" to "C. " They get stuck in traffic and become angry. They think the traffic jam made them upset. They don't realize that they don't HAVE to get angry. They skip an important step!

Let's try it again:

"A" —you get stuck in traffic.

"B" —you believe that you are given some unexpected and extra time to spend in **solitude**, to listen to a great tape or to plan your day.

"C" —the consequence is that you feel gratitude for the gift of time.

I have a friend who is fond of saying, "A traffic jam has no power to make us angry. It just stops our car. " He is aware that between the activating event and the consequence is something that we control : our beliefs about what is happening.

The next time you have a problem—at home or at work, big or small—decide to manage your attitude toward it. Practice the A-B-C method. You probably can't change "A", the **activating** event. But try hanging on "B", your beliefs about the problem. When you change your beliefs, you also change "C", the consequences of the situation.

It's as simple as A-B-C. Manage your beliefs, and you'll manage to be a lot happier!

佚 名

一个机场行李搬运员在航站楼边帮一个旅客搬行李时无意中撞翻了这个人的箱包。他赶快收拾起掉落的行李，并且为他的过失道歉。然而那个旅客一点不领情，他大发脾气，言辞激烈，粗暴地骂那个行李员笨拙。叫骂过程中，那个行李员始终都是微笑道歉。那个暴怒的旅客一直不停地训斥那个行李员，直到最后他去赶飞机。即使这样，那个行李员依然保持着平静和微笑。

排队等候的另一位顾客目睹了整个事件，对行李员的职业水准和控制力赞叹不已。"我从没见过如此的克制与谦卑。"他说，"当别人这么恶毒的攻击你时，你是怎么保持冷静的？"

"很简单。"行李员答道："他要去丹佛，但是他的行李会去底特律。"

这当然是一种处事的态度，但我们还有更富建设性的方法。

你听说过一个叫"A-B-C"的处事方法吗？这是个简单而有效的方法。

"A"表示"引发事件"。比如说你遇到交通堵塞，塞车就是那个引发事件。

"B"表示你的"信念系统"。你相信交通会越来越糟，以后像这样的日子会越来越多。

"C"代表"事件结果"。你开始生气，你想要鸣汽车喇叭，你的胃扭成了一团，你用拳头使劲砸仪表盘。

问题是……很多人会从"A"直接跳到"C"。他们遇到塞车就暴怒，他们认为塞车让他们难受，他们认识不到他们根本没必要愤怒，他们漏掉了最重要的一步。

我们来再试一遍：

"A"——你遇到塞车。

"B"——你认为你得到了意外的或额外的时间可以一个人待会儿，听听动听的音乐，或者计划一下一天的时间。

"C"——结果就是你会感激这份时间的礼物。

我有个朋友总喜欢说："塞车本身没有让我们发怒的魔力，它只是让车子停下来而已。"他知道在引发事件和结果之间的东西是我们所能控制的，即对于正在发生的事情的看法。

下次你遇到问题——无论在家里还是在单位，也无论大小——先决定你对这件事要采取什么态度。试试这个"A-B-C"法，也许你改变不了"A"，那个引发事件，但是试着把握"B"，你对这个问题的信念。当你改变了信念，你也就改变了"C"，事情的结果。

像 A-B-C 一样简单，掌握了你的信念，你就能获得更多的快乐！

Practising
& Exercise

核心单词

skycap ['skaikæp] *n.* 机场行李搬运工
mishap ['mishæp] *n.* 不幸事故；灾难
restraint [ris'treint] *n.* 抑制；控制；阻止
viciously ['viʃəsli] *adv.* 邪恶地；敌意地
solitude ['sɔlitjuːd] *n.* 孤独；寂寞；冷僻（处）；荒凉（之地）
activate ['æktiveit] *v.* 使活动起来

实用句型

Unappeased, the traveler burst into an angry tirade, raging and swearing at the skycap for his clumsiness. 然而那个旅客一点不领情，他大发脾气，言辞激烈，粗暴地骂那个行李员笨拙。

①现在分词 raging and swearing 在这里做状语，表伴随状态。

② burst into an angry 大发脾气，类似的表达还有 burst into tears 放声大哭；burst into the room 闯入房间等。

翻译行不行

1. 他把玻璃杯打翻了。(knocked over)

....

2. 字母 UN 代表什么？ (stand for)

....

3. 他很喜欢打篮球。(be fond of)

....

The Woman in the Mirror
镜中的女人

· Francis ·

When I was 11, I found out I had a brain tumor. I had surgery to remove it, but the size and location of the tumor caused my optic nerve to atrophy. For three years **afterward**, I had **partial** sight, but my ophthalmologist told me that eventually I would go blind. At the end of my 14th year, doctors pronounced me legally blind and said there was nothing that could be done. I had a 5 percent chance of surviving the tumor, and I did, but somehow I could never deal with the fact that I was going blind. I tried to behave as if everything were just fine. When it happened, I was **devastated**.

My dad left us when I was 15, and I took that really hard. Because of that, and because I was blind on top of it, my greatest fear was that no one was ever going to love me, that I would never get married and have kids and a full life. I was afraid of being alone, and I guess that is what I thought blindness meant.

Ten years later, on Nov. 16 of last year, I was cooking dinner and leaned over to kiss my guide dog, Ami. I lost my balance and hit my head on the corner of my coffee table and then on the floor. It wasn't unusual. When you are blind, you hit yourself all the time. I got up, finished making dinner and went to bed.

When I woke up, I could see. Light was coming through my window, and the curtains were drawn. Of course, I was shocked, but not **scared**, not like when I lost my sight. There is a big mirror in my bedroom, but I didn't look at myself right away. I wanted to wash my hair and put on make-up first. I do not look good in the morning, and I didn't want to be frightened. As I was showering, I caught my reflection. And that just that left me speechless, really.

The last time I saw myself, I had short hair, a pale complexion and features that didn't show because I had such light eyebrows and eyelashes I looked awful, like a **teenage** girl, I suppose Now, all of a sudden, I realized that it was true what people told me, that I was an attractive woman. *When I stood in front of the mirror, I reached to touch my face.* That is what I had been doing for 10 years— it was how I understood — so it was a natural impulse. It was not until I saw myself that I realized how much my memory had faded of things I once could see. It was about four hours before I told anyone. I stayed with Ami. We looked at each other and played outside in the yard. I just wanted to be alone, and take it in. It was so much.

The strange thing was that I knew it was going to happen. About a week before, I was walking Ami and suddenly saw blue dots in front of my left eye, the one I would regain my sight in. I told my mum because I found it funny ; blue had been my **favorite** color and was the easiest color for me to see when I had partial sight. I took it as a sign.

People don't treat me differently now. I was always completely independent. I lived in Auckland, New Zealand, in my own flat with my dog. I would have parties and go clubbing: I would listen to the beat of the music and go with it and hope for the best. When your friends grab you and point you in the other direction because they are actually over there, that is when you remember you're blind.

I also loved movies. Going to the movies blind was like someone telling you a really good story with great sound effects, and you make up all the images in your head. I haven't been back since I regained my sight. But I've been able to see my favorite soap, *Shortland Street*. And my friends took out magazines and pointed out Pamela Lee Anderson and Brad Pitt. The biggest surprise was Brad Pitt. I just thought, what is everyone going on about? The best was seeing my boyfriend. He rode the ferry over, and I knew him the moment I saw him. He was as sexy as I had imagined.

I am not surprised that things are pretty much the same in my life.I didn't expect anything more than what I have now. I worked very hard to surround myself with **genuine** people and to create a normal life for myself. I am still the same person. It just means that physically, perhaps, I can share more and put the two together, the feelings I had , with sight.

The same doctor who told me I would never see again told me I had regained 80 percent of the vision in my left eye. To be able to look him in the eye and tell him I could see again — honestly, that felt pretty damn good. He ran all the tests and made me read the eye chart, but he has no explanation. He said himself, and still says, that once the optic nerve is damaged, it cannot **regenerate**.

I don't think the knock on the head had anything to do with it. If others want to believe that is how it happened, that is fine. But I consider this a **miracle**. There is no other way to describe it. Some things just cannot be explained. Of course, some people are skeptical. For me, it is precious. I try not to think about the possibility of going blind again. But my recovery would be no less a miracle even if I lost my sight tomorrow.

弗兰克思

11 岁那年，我被诊断患有脑瘤。手术切除了脑瘤，但肿瘤的大小和位置却导致了我的视觉神经萎缩。3 年后，我还能看见一点点东西，但眼科医生说我最终会失明。快过完 14 岁时，医生断言我已经完全失明，并且毫无办法治疗。当时，我患上脑瘤后，存活的几率只有 5%，结果我活了下来，但对于即将失明的现实，我却无能为力。我努力表现得一切正常，但当它真正成为现实时，我却绝望了。

15 岁那年，父亲离开了我们，这简直令我无法承受。正因为如此，再加上处于失明最痛苦的时期，我最大的恐惧是没有人再爱我，我永远都不能结婚，不能有自己的孩子和一个完整的生活。我害怕孤独，我想，这些就是我当时对失明的理解。

10 年过去了，去年 11 月 16 日，我正在做晚餐，弯腰亲吻我的导盲犬阿米时，突然失去重心，一头撞在了咖啡桌的一角，然后又摔在地上。这没什么大不了的，要是你失明了，你也总会撞伤自己。我爬起来，继续做完晚餐，然后上床睡觉。

当我醒来时，我能看见了。阳光从拉着窗帘的窗户透进来。当然，我大吃一惊，但并不像失明时那样恐慌。卧室里挂着一面大镜子，我并没有立刻去照。我想先洗头，化妆，早晨的模样并不好看，我不想让自己受到惊吓。洗澡的时候，我看见了自己的影子。顿时说不出话来，真的。

最后一次见到自己时，我留着短短的头发，脸色苍白，面容黯淡。因为我的眉毛和睫毛都很淡，看起来像一个十几岁的小女孩，糟糕极了。但是，现在，我突然意识到，别人跟我说的都是真的，我是一个漂亮的女人。我站在镜子前，触摸着自己的脸。十年来，我一直这样做——我只是这样理解的——所以这是一种自然冲动。直到我看见自己，才意识到曾经看见的记忆，已经在很大程度上消退了。大约四个小时后，我才告诉其他人。我和阿米在一起，我们注视着对方，在外面的院子里的玩儿。我只想独自接受这一事实，它对我的意义太大了。

奇怪的是，我很早就知道自己会复明。大概一个星期前，我带着阿米散步，突然看见左眼前面有蓝色的圆点。后来正是这只眼睛复明了。我告诉了妈妈，因为很有趣的是，我一直最喜欢蓝色，这也是我还有部分视力时最容易看到的颜色。我把它当成了某种信号。

现在，我不再享有人们的特殊对待了，我一直独立生活，带着小狗住在新西兰奥克兰市自己的公寓里。我以前会参加聚会，去俱乐部玩，会听着音乐，打着节拍，祈求最佳状态。当我和朋友们一起疯玩时，只有当他们抓住我的手，指着另一个方向，告诉我，其实他们在那边时，我才想起自己是个盲人。

我也喜欢看电影，盲人看电影就好像在听别人给你讲一个非常好的故事，伴着精彩的音响效果，你可以在脑海中想象所有的情形。自从复明后，我还没有去看过电影，却在看我最喜欢的肥皂剧《苏特兰街》。朋友们翻开杂志，指着帕梅拉•李•安德森和布拉德•皮特给我看，布拉德•皮特最令我吃惊，我只是想，他有什么值得人们反复谈论的呢？最美妙的事是见到我的男朋友。他坐渡船过来，我一眼就认出了他，和我想象中的一样性感。

我并不感到惊奇，生活还和以前一样。现在拥有的一切已经让我感到很满足，我并不期望更多。我努力工作，置身于这些诚恳的人群中，为自己创造正常的生活。我还是以前的那个人，也许复明只是意味着，我能从身体上分享更多的东西，而且，能把以前的感受和现在的结合起来。

曾经说我再也不能复明的那个医生，现在又告诉我，我左眼的视力已经恢复了 80%。能够看着他，说我又能看见了——老实说，这感觉简直再好不过了。他给我做了所有的测试，让我读视力检查表，却没有做出任何解释，他依然像以前那样，自言自语道，视觉神经已经损坏了，不可能再生的。

我并不认为这和我那天撞到头有什么关系，如果别人要这样认为，那也没关系。但我认为这是一个奇迹，除此之外，再也没有其他方式可以形容了。有些事情就是无法解释。当然，有些人会很怀疑，但对我来说，它无比珍贵。我努力不去想可能还会失明，就是明天再度失明，我的恢复也依然是一个奇迹。

Practising

& Exercise 实战 提升篇

核心单词

afterward ['ɑ:ftəwəd] *adv.* 之后，以后，后来

partial ['pɑ:ʃəl] *adj.* 部分的，局部的；不完全的

devastate ['devəsteit] *v.* 使荒芜；破坏；使垮掉，压倒

scare [skɛə] *v.* 惊吓，使恐惧

teenage ['ti:neidʒ] *adj.* 十几岁的　*n.* 青少年时期

favorite ['feivərit] *adj.* 特别喜爱的

genuine ['dʒenjuin] *adj.* 真的；名副其实的；真诚的

regenerate [ri'dʒenərit] *adj.* 刷新的　*v.* 刷新；重建

miracle ['mirəkl] *n.* 奇迹；奇迹般的人（或物）

实用句型

when I stood in front of the mirror, I reached to touch my face.

我站在镜子前，触摸着自己的脸。

①时间状语从句：when 在这里表示"就是这时"。

② in front of 在……的前面，类似的表达还有 in the front of 位于……的前部；in view of 鉴于，考虑到；in terms of 就……而论，在……方面等固定搭配。

翻译行不行

1. 他们忍无可忍了。(at the end of)

....

2. 这本书论及一个重要的问题。(deal with)

....

3. 他指出了我的错误。(point out)

....

The Secret of Happiness
幸福的秘诀

• Anonymous •

Once there lived a king of great **strength** and wealth. Yet he was not happy. He told his servants to find him things to make him happy, but each came back saying, *"Nothing in the world can match the wonderful things you have already."* Then in that land, there lived a poor man with a **patch** over one eye and a **crutch** to help him walk. Although he had little, he was always happy. When the king heard of this, he asked the man to teach him his **secret**.

"I never **push**," the man replied, "and I never rush. Most of all, I never wish for too much." Then he smiled and was gone.

If you would make a man happy, do not add to his possessions but subtract from his desires.

佚 名

从前有一位国王，很有权力和财富，然而他并不快乐。他告诉仆人去找可以使他快乐的东西，但是每个回来的人都说："世界上没有什么比你已经拥有的再好的东西了。"当时那个国家住着一个穷人，他一个眼睛戴着眼罩并靠拐杖走路。虽然他拥有的很少，但是他总是很快乐。当国王听说这件事的时候，便要求这个人教他快乐的秘诀。

"我从不强迫，"这个人答道，"而且我从不匆忙。最重要的是，我从不希望得到太多。"然后，他笑着离开了。

如果你想让一个人快乐，不要增加他的财产，而是要减少他的欲望。

核心单词

strength [streŋθ] *n.* 力量；效力；长处

patch [pætʃ] *n.* 补钉，补片；贴片

crutch [krʌtʃ] *n.* 支撑物，支持，依靠

secret ['si:krit] *adj.* 秘密的，私下的

rush [rʌʃ] *v.* 冲，奔，仓促行动

实用句型

Nothing in the world can match the wonderful things you have already.

世界上没有什么比你已经拥有的再好的东西了。

① Nothing 放在句首时，要用倒装语序。

② match 敌得过，比得上，类似的表达还有 match against 使较量，使比赛；match up（使）相配等固定搭配。

翻译行不行

1. 短裙子又开始流行了。（come back）

....

2. 恶劣的天气增加了我们的困难。（add to）

....

3.7 减 2 等于 5。（subtract from）

....

生活就像一盒 **巧克力**

Life was like a box of chocolates

The Daffodil Principle
水仙定律

Jaroldeen Edwards •

Several times my daughter had telephoned to say, "Mother, you must come see the daffodils before they are over. " I wanted to go, but it was a two-hour drive from Laguna to Lake Arrowhead.

"I will come next Tuesday. " I promised, a little **reluctantly**, on her third call. Next Tuesday dawned cold and rainy. Still, I had promised, and so I drove there. When I finally walked into Carolyn's house and hugged and greeted my grandchildren, I said, "Forget the daffodils, Carolyn! The road is **invisible** in the clouds and fog, and there is nothing in the world except you and these children that I want to see badly enough to drive another inch! "

My daughter smiled calmly and said, "We drive in this all the time, Mother."

"Well, you won't get me back on the road until it clears, and then I'm heading for home!" I assured her.

"I was hoping you'd take me over to the garage to pick up my car.

"How far will we have to drive?"

"Just a few blocks," Carolyn said, "I'll drive. I'm used to this."

After several minutes, I had to ask, "Where are we going? This isn't the way to the garage!" "We're going to my garage the long way," Carolyn smiled, "by way of the daffodils."

"Carolyn," I said **sternly**, "please turn around."

"It's all right, Mother, I promise. You will never forgive yourself if you miss this experience."

After about twenty minutes, we turned onto a small gravel road and I saw a small church. On the far side of the church, I saw a hand-lettered sign that read, "Daffodil Garden".

We got out of the car and each took a child's hand, and I followed Carolyn down the path. Then, we turned a corner of the path, and I looked up and gasped. Before me lay the most glorious sight. It looked as though someone had taken a great vat of gold and poured it down over the mountain peak and slopes. The flowers were planted in **majestic**, swirling patterns—great ribbons and swaths of deep orange, white, lemon yellow, salmon pink, saffron, and butter yellow. Each different-colored variety was planted as a group so that it swirled and flowed like its own river with its own unique hue. There were five acres of flowers.

"But who has done this?" I asked Carolyn.

"It's just one woman." Carolyn answered. "She lives on the property. That's her home." Carolyn pointed to a well-kept A-frame house that looked small and modest in the midst of all that glory. We walked up to the house. On the patio, we saw a poster. "Answers to the Questions I Know You Are Asking" was the **headline**.

The first answer was a simple one. "50, 000 bulbs. " it read.

The second answer was, "one bulb at a time, by one woman. Two hands, two feet, and a very little brain".

The third answer was, "Began in 1958".

There it was. The Daffodil Principle. For me, that moment was a life-changing experience. I thought of this woman whom I had never met, who, more than thirty-five years before, had begun—one bulb at a time—to bring her vision of beauty and joy to an **obscure** mountain top.

Just planting one bulb at a time, year after year, this unknown woman had forever changed the world in which she lived. *She had created something of ineffable magnificence, beauty, and inspiration.*

The principle her daffodil garden taught is one of the greatest principles of celebration. That is, learning to move toward our goals and desires one step at a time often just one baby-step at a time—and learning to love the doing, learning to use the accumulation of time. When we multiply tiny pieces of time with small **increments** of daily effort, we too will find we can accomplish magnificent things. We can change the world.

"It makes me sad in a way. " I admitted to Carolyn. 'What might I have accomplished if I had thought of a wonderful goal thirty-five years ago and had worked away at it 'one bulb at a time' through all those years? Just think what I might have been able to achieve!"

My daughter summed up the message of the day in her direct way. "Start tomorrow." she said.

贾洛德·爱德华思

好几次了，我女儿打电话来说："妈妈，你务必得在那些水仙花凋谢之前来看看它们。"我是想去，可从拉古娜到箭头湖要开两个小时的车。

"那我下周二去吧。"在她第三次打来电话时，我极不情愿地答应道。到了那个周二，清晨很冷又下着雨，不过既然答应了，我还是开车去了。等我终于到了卡罗琳家，拥抱问候过我的外孙们，说："卡罗琳，别想那水仙了！天阴又有雾，路都看不清。这世上除了你和这些孩子，没有什么能让我为想去看他们再开一步车了！"

女儿平静地笑着说："妈妈，我们一直都在这种天气里开车的呀！"

"那反正你甭想让我再开车上路了，除非天晴了，然后我就直接开车回家！"我重申道。

"我本来指望你能开车捎我去修车厂取我的车呢！"

"我们得开多远啊？"

"就几条街，"卡罗琳说，"我来开，反正我习惯了这种天气。"

过了几分钟，我不得不问："我们这是去哪儿啊？这不是去修车厂的路啊！"卡罗琳笑了，"我们要去的那个修车厂很远，要经过水仙花。"

"卡罗琳，"我严厉地说，"请你掉头回去。"

"没事的，妈妈，我保证。如果你错过了这次经历，你永远不会原谅自己的。"

大概过了 20 分钟，我们转到了一条碎石小路上，我看到一个小教堂。在教堂的稍远一侧，我看见一个手写的牌子，上面写着："水仙花园"。

我们走下车，一人领着一个孩子。我跟着卡罗琳顺小道而行，转到小道的一角，我抬头一看，惊住了。在我面前是极为壮观的景象，看上去仿佛有人把一大缸金子倾倒下来，覆盖了峰顶和山坡。那些花栽种成宏伟的漩涡图案——宽宽窄窄的条纹有很多颜色，有深橘、白、柠檬黄、橙红、番红和乳黄。每种不同色系的多种颜色种植为一组，这样看上去每组都用自己独特的色调一圈圈地在自己的河流中流淌。那有五亩花。

"这是谁种的呢？"我问卡罗琳。

"就一个女人，"卡罗琳回答，"她就以这片花为生。那是她的家。"卡罗琳指着一个整修得很好的 A 字形房子，在一片壮丽的景象当中，这房子看起来小而朴素。我走到房子跟前，在院子里，我看到一张海报，标题是"答案——我知道你要问的这些问题"。

第一个答案很简单，写着："50,000 株"。

第二个答案是："一次种一株，一个女人，两只手，两只脚，不需多动脑"。

第三个答案是："开始于 1958 年"。

这就是"水仙定律"。对于我,那一刻是一次改变生活的经历。我在琢磨这个我从未谋面的女人,她,在 35 年前,开始——一次种一株——给她自己带来了美的景象和花满山顶的快乐。

　　就这样一次种一株,年复一年,这个不知名的女人永远地改变了她所居住的世界,她创造了无法形容的壮丽、美好和感动。

　　在这个水仙花园中得出的定律是值得庆祝的最伟大的定律之一。那就是,懂得向我们的目标迈进,只求一步一个脚印——通常一次就一小步——懂得去热爱正在做的事,懂得利用时间的积累。当我们把时间的碎片叠加,再加上每天的一点努力,我们会发现我们也能成就辉煌。我们也能改变这个世界。

　　"这让我在某种意义上有点丧气。"我跟卡罗琳说,"如果我 35 年前有一个宏伟的目标,然后也像这样,'一次种一株'地做下去,这些年我会有什么成就呢?想想我到底能做成什么!"

　　女儿直截了当地总结了那天的收获。她说:"从明天开始。"

生活就像一盒巧克力

核心单词

reluctantly [ri'lʌktəntli] *adv.* 不情愿地；勉强地

invisible [in'vizəbl] *adj.* 看不见的；无形的

sternly ['stə:nli] *adv.* 严格地；严厉地

majestic [mə'dʒestik] *adj.* 雄伟的；威严的

headline ['hedlain] *n.* (报纸等的)标题；大标题

obscure [əb'skjuə] *adj.* 黑暗的；朦胧的；晦涩的

increment ['inkrimənt] *n.* 增加；增额

实用句型

She had created something of ineffable magnificence, beauty, and inspiration. 她创造了无法形容的壮丽、美好和感动。

①过去完成时：had+P.P(动词的过去分词)。

② ineffable 说不出的，类似带有否定前缀的词还有 imbalance 不均衡状态；illegal 非法的；irresponsible 不负责任的等。

翻译行不行

1. 他昨晚到十二点才睡觉。(not until)

......

2. 我们在大雨中离去。(in the midst of)

......

3. 所有这些都说明了同样的结论。(point to)

......

A Turtle Brought Me "Enlightenment"
一只让我悟道的乌龟

• Michael Chase •

Life is good, really good. Sometimes I feel like the good karma train picks me up, and simply refuses to let me off. I have an amazing wife, a teenage son that makes me glow with pride, good health, a wonderful family and the best friends a guy could ask for. I have a lot to be grateful for. For many years now, "thank you" has become my **meditation** as I start each day.

But the truth is, life was not always this good. It wasn't all that long ago, when the resume of my life looked radically different. At one time, my life was filled with nearly everything that people try to avoid. Experiencing everything from unhappy relationships to financial struggles, poor health, depression, and an endless stream of negative habits was a part of my daily life. It seemed that no matter how hard I tried, happiness was constantly eluding me and disappointment became my shadow. It also seemed as if I was paving the way for a future that sadly resembled my father's, until he took his own life at the age of 54. This was a defining moment for me. Once the shock of losing my father began to fade, **clarity** and a new sense of purpose became the dominant force in my life. I remember feeling as if I had "met myself" for the very first time while also became conscious of my life's true purpose. It was in that moment that I had made a major decision. *Not only would I change my own life, but I would also make a difference in the lives of others.*

Enlightenment and **epiphanies** can show up in some pretty strange ways. The Buddha found it under a Boddhi tree, Nelson Mandela in prison and spiritual guru Ram Dass through psychedelic drugs. Little did I know, mine would arrive in the form of a hard-shelled reptile simply trying to cross the road— a turtle.

But this wasn't just any turtle, this was the world's most optimistic one. He was **tenaciously** determined to cross twenty feet of tar as cars zoomed by at 55 mph. But today was his lucky day. My wife's quick reflexes not only ensured that "turtle soup" would not be for dinner that night, but her act of kindness would eventually become the foundation for everything I teach today. As unusual as this sounds, the simple act of pulling our car over, removing this little turtle from harms way, and placing him back into the wild, caused something extraordinary to happen inside of me. As I stood there holding this tiny creature in my hands, a wave of pure joy came over me. It was that warm, teary-eyed sensation that we feel during life's greatest moments ; like falling in love or the birth of a child. I honestly felt as if my heart was completely opening up as everything stood still around me. In no way would I have described it as "enlightenment", but there was no doubt about it—helping this little turtle just felt so damn good! But why? After all, it was just a turtle, right?

And then it hit me. I finally realized what was happening. At that point, a flood of inspiring thoughts surged through me. I walked back to the car, opened my journal and wrote eight words that would later prove to be life changing for me: "kindness creates happiness" and "live a life of kindness". It was the answer I had been looking for. The secret to inner peace and lasting happiness was kindness. Not "random acts of " or simply being nice, but rather as a way of life. I had already known the benefits of kindness through studying many eastern philosophies, but I had never actually considered it as a lifestyle.

But, this day was just beginning.

Just thirty minutes after my mini-epiphany, my wife and I arrived at our original destination—a country garden show. After walking around for just a few minutes, a gentle faced 60-something looking man waved me over to the front porch of his farmhouse, for no apparent reason. The entire setting was like a scene out of an old movie—weathered rocking chairs—the smell of cookies baking—and a coon cat that looked as old as the farmhouse itself. "Let her look around. Come and sit with me." he said.

I had no idea what to expect, but as I sunk into the large wicker chair beside him, I couldn't help feeling that he was going to say something profound. After all, if a turtle can change my life, why not a wise old farmer? After a brief hello and a polite introduction, we simply sat in silence and let the sunlight warm our faces. After what seemed like an **eternity**, he finally spoke. "You know," he said, "I've often thought that the meaning of life is making things a little bit easier for those around us, what do you think?" I was speechless. It felt like I had just been hit on the head again by life's big karma stick. He went on to tell me his **version** of "the secrets to life" and how "true happiness can only be found by loving and serving others". Finally he finished with "Oh, and don't forget you really gotta' love the one you're with yourself".

Life was obviously trying to tell me something. In the days and weeks that followed, the world looked completely different to me. The more I studied and tested my "kindness creates happiness" theory, the more I was blown away by its life-changing power. I realized that most of my disappointments in life were simply because I had been unkind to others and especially to myself.

After spending much of my life thinking "What's in it for me?", my new inner **mantra** became "Am I being kind?" This one simple question changed my life. So, whenever I feel the need to disagree with my wife, lash out at a rude employee in the mall or even before I shove ten cookies into my mouth, I go within and ask, "Am I being kind?" These four little words have become my source to inner peace. It has created many positive changes in me such as recycling and acting more "green" and consciously respecting all of life. I even stopped setting the mousetraps in the garage. (My wife is going to kill me when she reads that last one.) Another big change in my life was the irresistible urge to perform "**spontaneous** acts of kindness". Things like buying coffee for strangers and giving money to the homeless just seemed natural. Each kind act felt like a blissful surge of energy through my chest. But what became even more **exhilarating** were the intense feelings of warmth towards everyone around me—especially difficult people. Whether there was someone who acted rude in traffic or an inconsiderate person in line at the grocery store，I no longer felt anxious or offended— I simply wished for their happiness. That's when I realized what it truly meant to be living kindness.

All thanks to an unexpected turtle crossing the street that day.

麦克·驰思

生活不错，很不错。有时我觉得仿佛坐上了一列善有善报的列车，想下车都不行。我有个人人夸好的妻子，有个给我脸上增光的十几岁的儿子，我们身体健康，家庭美满和睦，还有一帮世上最棒的朋友。我有好多值得感恩的东西。多年来，"感谢老天"已经成了我开始每一天的默祷词。

可是事实上，生活并不总是这么美好。就在不久前，我的人生简历看上去还是迥然不同。曾经一度，我的生活充满了令每个人都想躲避的东西。从让人沮丧的婚姻，到困窘的经济状况，糟糕的健康，抑郁的心情和无穷无尽的坏毛病，都是我每天生活的一部分。似乎不管我怎么努力，快乐总是躲着我走，而失望则如影随形。而且似乎我在亦步亦趋地把日子过成父亲那样，他在 54 岁的时候自杀了。那一刻成了我人生的转折点，一度失去父亲所受的打击开始消退，慈善和生活的目标感开始支配我的生活。我觉着好像有生以来第一次发现了自己，认识到了生命的真正目的。从那一刻起，我便做了一个重大决定。我不仅要改变自己的生活，而且要令别人的生活改观。

令人茅塞顿开的灵光会以相当奇特的方式出现。佛祖在菩提树下悟道；纳尔逊•曼德拉在狱中觉醒；灵魂大师瑞姆•达斯则在致幻剂中获得升华。我从未曾料到，我的启示会以一只试图穿越马路的硬壳爬行动物的形象出现，它是一只乌龟。

但这可不是一只普通的乌龟，这是世上最乐观的一只乌龟。它不屈不挠地打算穿越一条宽 20 英尺的柏油马路，路上是川流不息的以时速 55 英里行驶的车辆。可是今天是它的幸运日。我妻子的快速反应不仅保证了它不会以"乌龟汤"的形式成为今晚的餐桌一景，而且她接下来的善举还成就了我今天要讲述的一切的基础。这听上去要多玄有多玄，一个简单的将车停到路边，把这只小乌龟救离险境并将之归还给大自然的举动引发了我内心深处一场惊天动地的变革。当我站在那里，手捧着这个小生命，一种纯粹的喜悦感席卷了我。那是一种温暖的催人泪下的感觉，往往发生在人生最伟大的时刻，比如坠入爱河，比如婴儿降生。

我真的觉得我的心完完全全地向着我周围静止的万物开启。我不想把这称之为"启示",但它又千真万确就是——帮助这只小乌龟感觉真是太棒了!可是,为什么会这样?它终究不过是一只乌龟嘛,是吧?

然后事情发生了。我终于明白自己顿悟到了什么。彼时彼刻,思想的潮水汹涌而至。我走回车里,打开笔记本,写下 8 个字,事后证明这 8 个字成为了我的人生转折点:"善生乐",以及"人生须行善"。这就是我孜孜以求的答案。内心宁静和永远快乐的奥秘就是善。不是"偶尔为之"或简单发发善心,而是变成一种生活方式。我已经通过研究许多东方哲学知道了善的妙处,但从没想过要把它变成一种生活方式。

可是,这一天来临了。

就在我小小顿悟完毕的 30 分钟后,我和妻子到了原定的目的地,那是一个乡村花园展览所。四处走了一小会儿,一个 60 岁左右的慈眉善目的男人在他的农舍门前向我挥手,好像没什么明显的理由。这一幕完全像是老电影中的场景:老旧的摇椅,烘烤糕点的气息,一只看上去和农舍一样老的长毛猫。"让她随意走走,你过来坐坐。"他说。

我不知道将要发生什么,但当我坐进他身旁那张宽大的藤椅里,不由觉得他会对我说些意味深长的话。毕竟,要是一只乌龟都能改变我的人生,为什么一个睿智的老农不能呢?简单寒暄之后,我们都静静地坐着,阳光温暖地照着脸庞。好像过了一辈子那么久,他终于开口了。"你瞧,"他说,"我常以为,生命的意义是让周围的人过得好一点,你说呢?"我哑口无言。好像脑袋上又挨了人生的一记闷棍。他继续跟我说起他理解的

"人生奥秘"，和"真正的快乐只能从关爱和服务他人中获得"。最后他说，"噢，别忘了……你必须得爱你与之相伴的那个人，就是你自己。"

显然，生活会让我领悟到些什么。随后的几天和几个星期，整个世界在我眼中完全变了模样。我越是研究和验证我的"善生乐"理论，我越是为它那改变人生的力量所倾倒。我发现生活中绝大多数失望都是源于我对别人的不善，尤其是对自己的不善。

花了大半辈子琢磨人生的意义，我的新灵魂咒语变成，"我有没有为善？"这个简单的问题改变了我的生活。当我想和妻子争论的时候，当我想对粗鲁的商店售货员训斥的时候，甚至当我想往嘴巴里狂塞饼干的时候，我都会自问，"我有没有为善？"这几个字成为我内心平静的源泉。它在我内心生出许多好的变化，比如循环再利用资源，做环保人士，而且有意识地尊重一切事物。我甚至不再在车库里安置捕鼠器（我妻子要是读到这最后一句可能会杀了我）。另一个大变化是我控制不住地要去做"自然而然的善行"。比如给陌生人买咖啡，把零钱给流浪汉等，这样的行为做起来是那么自然。每个善行都好似一股幸福的能量在我胸膛里汹涌澎湃。但最让人愉快的是对我周围每一个人的强烈的亲切感，尤其是对那些坏脾气的人。不管是粗野无礼的司机，还是食品店排队加塞的家伙，我不再觉得焦灼不安或是怒不可遏，我只是希望他们能快乐。那是当我明白了人生须行善的真意之后。

所有这一切，都要归功于那天的一只不期而至穿过马路的乌龟。

Practising

& Exercise

实战
提升篇

核心单词

animated ['ænimeitid] *adj.* 栩栩如生的；活跃的；热烈的

sensation [sen'seiʃən] *n.* 感觉，知觉

generous ['dʒenərəs] *adj.* 慷慨的，大方的

delicious [di'liʃəs] *adj.* 美味的；香喷喷的

fabulous ['fæbjuləs] *adj.* 惊人的；难以置信的

talented ['tæləntid] *adj.* 有天才的，有才干的

flashing ['flæʃiŋ] *n.* 闪光；闪烁

fade [feid] *v.* 凋谢，枯萎

实用句型

She was almost out of breath when she reached out and softly touched my arm. 当她伸手轻轻抚摸我的臂膀时，已经奄奄一息了。

①这里是由 when 引导的时间状语从句。

② reach out 伸出，类似的表达还有 out of reach 够不着；reach for 伸手去拿等固定搭配。

翻译行不行

1. 此房年久失修。（used to）

....

2. 太阳一出来，雾就会消失了。（pass away）

....

3. 幸亏有你了的帮忙，我们才得以按时完成任务。（thanks to）

....

Keep Walking in Sunshine
一直走在阳光里

• Anonymous •

Years of storms had taken their toll on the old windmill. Its wheel, rusted and fallen, lay silently in the lush bluegrass. Its once **animated** silhouette was now a tall motionless steeple in the twilight sun.

I hadn't walked across our old farm in fifteen years. Yet the **sensations** came flooding back. I could smell the freshness of new mown alfalfa. I could feel the ping of the ice cold summer rain, and the sun's sudden warmth on my wet shoulders when it reappeared after a brisk July thunderstorm.

Rain or shine, I used to walk this path each day to see Greta. She always made me smile, even after Sis and I had just had a big squabble. I would help Greta with her chores. Then we would visit over a **generous** helping of her **delicious** homemade chocolate cookies and ice cream. Being confined to a wheel chair didn't stop Greta from being a **fabulous** cook.

Greta gave me two of the greatest gifts I've ever received. First, she taught me how to read. She also taught me that when I forgave Sis for our squabbles, it meant I wouldn't keep feeling like a victim. Instead, I would feel sunny.

Mr. Dinking, the local banker, tried to foreclose on Greta's house and land after her husband passed away. Thanks to Pa and Uncle Johan, Greta could keep everything. Pa said that it was the least he could do for someone **talented** enough to teach me to read!

Soon folks were coming from miles around to buy Greta's homemade cakes, pies, breads, cookies, cider, and ice cream. Hank, the grocery store man, came each week to stock his shelves and bring Greta supplies.

Greta even had me take a big apple pie to Mr. Dinking who became one of her best customers and friends. That's just how Greta was. She could turn anyone into a friend!

Greta always said, "Dear, keep walking in sunshine!" No matter how terrible my day started, I always felt sunny walking home from Greta's house—even beneath the winter starlight.

I arrived at Greta's house today just after sunset. An ambulance had stopped a few feet from her door, its red lights **flashing**. When I ran into the old house, Greta recognized me right away.

She smiled at me with her unforgettable twinkling blue eyes. *She was almost out of breath when she reached out and softly touched my arm.* Her last words to me were "Dear, keep walking in sunshine!"

I'm sure that Greta is walking in the brightest sunshine she's ever seen. And, I'm sure that she heard every word I read at her memorial service. I chose a beautiful verse by Leo Buscaglia. It's one that Greta taught me to read many years ago...

"Love can never grow old. Locks may lose their brown and gold. Cheeks may **fade** and hollow grow. But the hearts that love will know, never winter's frost and chill, summer's warmth is in them still."

佚 名

　　多年的风雨侵蚀了古老的风车。车轮锈了，掉了，静静地躺卧在茂盛的蓝色禾草中。落日余晖下，风车那一度生机勃勃的形象如今变成了死气沉沉的高大尖塔。

　　我已经有 15 年没有步行穿过我们的农场了，然而，昔日感觉如潮水般卷来。我又闻到了新割苜蓿的清新味道，感受到了夏天的冰冷雨滴敲打在身上，还有七月雷雨后，太阳重现天际，被打湿的肩膀上瞬间便能感到的温暖。

　　曾经无论晴雨，我天天沿着这条小径去探望葛丽塔，即使我刚和姐姐大吵了一场，葛丽塔也总能使我开心起来。我会帮葛丽塔做些杂事，然后，我们会大吃她亲手做的美味巧克力曲奇饼和冰淇淋。尽管她坐在轮椅上，但并不妨碍葛丽塔成为一名出色的厨师。

　　葛丽塔送给我两件我有生以来收到的最棒的礼物。首先，她教会我认字。另外，葛丽塔还让我懂得，不再记恨和姐姐的争吵而原谅她时，可以使我自己不再觉得像个受害者，相反，宽恕会令我心情开朗。

在葛丽塔的丈夫去世后，当地的银行家丁肯先生要收取她抵押给银行的房子和土地。幸亏有爸爸和约翰叔叔的帮忙，葛丽塔才保住了一切。爸爸说，对一位本领高强到居然能够教会我认字的人，这只是他力所能及的一件小事！

很快，方圆数英里的人们都来买葛丽塔自制的蛋糕、馅饼、面包、曲奇饼、苹果酒和冰淇淋。每个礼拜，杂货店老板汉克都会来这里进货，并带给她新的材料。

葛丽塔甚至让我给丁肯先生送去一个大大的苹果馅饼，他后来也成了她最好的顾客和朋友之一。这就是葛丽塔，她能把所有人都变成朋友！

葛丽塔总说："亲爱的，要一直走在阳光里！"不管这一天是多么的糟糕，从葛丽塔的小屋走回家时，即使头顶上是冬夜的星光，我都觉得心情无比灿烂。

这天，我来到葛丽塔家时，太阳刚下山，她门外几英尺处停着一辆救护车，车上的红灯不住闪烁。当我冲入那所老房子时，葛丽塔立刻认出了我。

她冲我微笑着，那双令人难忘的蓝眼睛闪着光芒。当她伸出手轻轻抚摸我的臂膀时，已经奄奄一息了。她最后对我说的话是："亲爱的，要一直走在阳光里！"

我肯定葛丽塔此时正走在前所未有的灿烂阳光里，我还肯定她听见了我在她的追思仪式上所念的每一个字。我选了里欧·巴斯卡格利亚的一首优美的诗，那是多年前葛丽塔曾经教我念的……

"爱永不会老。锁头会锈蚀，红颜会消退。只要心中有爱，严冬便永不降临，夏日的温暖永驻。"

核心单词

meditation [medi'teiʃən] *n.* 沉思，默想；冥想

clarity ['klæriti] *n.* 清楚；明晰；清澈

epiphany [i'pifəni] *n.* 显现；顿悟

tenaciously [ti'neiʃəsli] *adv.* 坚持地；顽强地

eternity [i(:)'tə:niti] *n.* 永远，永恒；来世；永恒的真理

version ['və:ʃən] *n.* 译文；译本

mantra ['mʌntrə] *n.* 真言；（印度教、大乘佛教中的）祈祷文

spontaneous [spɔn'teinjəs] *adj.* 自发的；无意识的，不由自主的

exhilarate [ig'ziləreit] *v.* 使振奋；使高兴

实用句型

Not only would I change my own life, but I would also make a difference in the lives of others.

我不仅要改变自己的生活，而且要令别人的生活改观。

① not only 放在句首时，第一个句子要部分倒装。

② make a difference 有所区别，类似的表达还有 make some difference 有些区别；make no difference 没有区别；make all the difference 大不相同等。

翻译行不行

1. 请你明天上午到机场接我。（pick up）

....

2. 学校应该培养学生的责任感。（a sense of ）

....

3. 听到汶川糟糕的情况，我忍不住哭了。（could not help）

....

say, "we will turn giddy."

We seem so frightened today of being alone that we never let it happen. *Even if family, friends and movies should fail, there is still the radio or television to fill up the void.* Women, who used to complain of loneliness, need never be alone any more. We can do our housework with soap-opera heroes at our side. Even day-dreaming was more **creative** than this; it demanded something of oneself and it fed the inner life. Now instead of planting our solitude with our dream blossoms, we choke the space with **continuous** music, chatter and companionship to which we do not even listen. It is simply there to fill the vacuum. When the noise stops there is no inner music to take its place. We must relearn to be alone.

埃 文

岛屿是多么奇妙啊！它处在一望无际之中，四周海水围绕，没有桥梁相通，没有电缆相连，更无电话可打。我来的小岛就是这样一个地方，它远离尘世，不见喧嚣。小岛是时间的孤岛，就像我的这次短期假期。在这里，过去和未来都被隔断，只有现时依然存在。一个人，或是像个孩子，或是像个圣人，现在便实实在在地在这里活着。每一天、每一个动作其实都是一个小岛，经受着时间和空间的冲刷，像小岛一样完美。人在这种环境下也变成了小岛，独立自主，完整安详，尊重他人的孤独，不践踏他人的海岸半步，毕恭毕敬地在他人的奇迹面前靠后站。"没有人会是小岛。"约翰·多恩说过。我却认为每个人都是公共海域的小岛。

归根结底，我们都是孤独的。这种孤独的基本状态由不得我们选择。奥地利诗人里尔克曾经说道："由不得我们带走或是放弃。"虽然身心孤独，但是我们都欺骗自己，假装事实并非如此。里尔克还说，"我们很自然就会弄得头晕目眩。"

今天的人们都非常害怕孤独，所以极力避免它。当与家人和朋友相处或是看电影都无法消除孤独的时候，我们就用听广播和看电视来填补空白。女人们曾经埋怨孤独，现在想孤独也办不到。她们可以一边做家务一边看肥皂剧。做白日梦都显得更有创造力，它需要人们具有一些东西，而且能够丰富内心生活。我们本该用白日梦的似锦繁花来种下一片孤独，但却用连续不断的音乐、喋喋不休、吵嚷的同伴来把孤独的空间堵死。这其实仅仅是一个填补空缺的问题，一旦喧闹消失，便不再有内心的音乐来填补空缺。我们要重新学会孤独。

Practising **实战**
& Exercise 提升篇

核心单词

saint [seint] *n.* 圣徒；虔诚的人

reverence ['revərəns] *n.* 敬爱，崇敬

miracle ['mirəkl] *n.* 奇迹；奇迹般的人

analysis [ə'nælisis] *n.* 分析；分解

solitude ['sɔlitjuːd] *n.* 孤独；寂寞

delude [di'luːd] *v.* 欺骗；哄骗

creative [kri(ː)'eitiv] *adj.* 创造的；有创造力

continuous [kən'tinjuəs] *adj.* 连续的，不断的

实用句型

Even if family, friends and movies should fail, there is sitll the radio or television to fill up the void. 当与家人和朋友相处或是看电影都无法消除孤独的时候，我们就用听广播和看电视来填补空白。

① even if 即使，在这里引导让步状语从句。

② fill up 装满，被填满，类似的表达还有 fill in 填写，代替；fill with 充满；fill out 变丰满，填写等固定搭配。

翻译行不行

1. 我在打长途时，电话线突然被切断了。(cut off)

......

2. 他在这个谈判中做中间人。(act as)

......

3. 对她而言，Tom 永远无法代替 John。(take the place)

......

Advice to Youth
给年轻人的忠告

• Donald •

Being told I would be expected to talk here, I inquired what sort of talk I ought to make. They said it should be something suitable to youth—something **didactic**, instructive, or something in the nature of good advice. Very well. I have a few things in my mind which I have often longed to say for the instruction of the young ; for it is in one's tender early years that such things will best take root and be most enduring and most valuable. First, then. I will say to you my young friends—and I say it **beseechingly**, urgingly.

Always obey your parents, when they are present. This is the best policy in the long run, because if you don't, they will make you. Most parents think they know better than you do, and you can generally make more by humoring that superstition than you can by acting on your own better judgment.

Be respectful to your superiors, if you have any, also to strangers, and sometimes to others. If a person offend you, and you are in doubt as to whether it was intentional or not, do not resort to extreme measures ; simply watch your chance and hit him with a brick. That will be sufficient. If you shall find that he had not intended any offense, come out frankly and confess yourself in the wrong when you struck him ; acknowledge it like a man and say you didn't mean to. Yes, always avoid violence ; in this age of charity and kindliness, the time has gone by for such things, Leave **dynamite** to the low and unrefined.

Go to bed early, get up early — *this is wise*. Some authorities say get up with the sun ; some say get up with one thing, others with another. But a lark is really the best thing to get up with. It gives you a **splendid** reputation with everybody to know that you get up with the lark ; and if you get the right kind of lark, and work at him right, you can easily train him to get up at half past nine, every time—it's no trick at all.

Now as to the matter of lying. You want to be very careful about lying ; otherwise you are nearly sure to get caught. Once caught, you can never again be, in the eyes of the good and the pure, what you were before. Many a young person has injured himself **permanently** through a single clumsy and ill finished lie, the result of carelessness born of incomplete training. Some authorities hold that the young out not to lie at all. That of course, is putting it rather stronger than necessary ; still, while I cannot go quite so far as that, I do maintain, and I believe I am right, that the young ought to be temperate in the use of this great art until practice and experience shall give them that confidence, elegance, and precision which alone can make the accomplishment graceful and profitable. Patience, diligence, painstaking attention to detail—these are requirements ; these in time, will make the student perfect ; upon these only, may he rely as the sure foundation for future eminence. Think what **tedious** years of study, thought, practice, experience, went to the equipment of that peerless old master who was able to impose upon the whole world the lofty and sounding maxim that "Truth is mighty and will prevail" — the most **majestic** compound fracture of fact which any of woman born has yet achieved. For the history of our race, and each individual's experience, are sewn thick with evidences that a truth is not hard to kill, and that a lie well told is immortal. There is in Boston a monument of the man who discovered anesthesia ; many people are aware, in these latter days, that that man didn't discover it at all, but stole the discovery from another man. Is this truth mighty, and will it prevail? Ah no, my hearers, the monument is made of hardy material, but the lie it tells will outlast it a million years. An awkward, feeble, leaky lie is a thing which you ought to make it your unceasing study to avoid ; such a lie as that has no more real permanence than an average truth. Why, you might as well tell the truth at once and be done with it. A feeble, stupid, preposterous lie will not live two years—except it be a slander upon somebody. It is indestructible, then, of course, but that is no merit of yours. A final word: begin your practice of this gracious and beautiful art early—begin now. If I had begun earlier, I could have learned how.

Never handle firearms carelessly. The sorrow and suffering that have been caused through the innocent but heedless handling of firearms by the young! Only four days ago, right in the next farm house to the one where I am spending the summer, a grandmother, old and gray and sweet, one of the loveliest spirits in the land, was sitting at her work, when her young grandson crept in and got down an old, battered, rusty gun which had not been touched for many years and was supposed not to be loaded, and pointed it at her, laughing and threatening to shoot. In her **fright** she ran screaming and pleading toward the door on the other side of the room ; but as she passed him he placed the gun almost against her very breast and pulled the trigger! He had supposed it was not loaded. And he was right— it wasn't. So there wasn't any harm done. It is the only case of that kind I ever heard of. Therefore, just the same, don't you meddle with old unloaded firearms ; they are the most deadly and unerring things that have ever been created by man. You don't have to take any pains at all with them ; you don't have to have a rest, you don't have to have any sights on the gun, you don't have to take aim, even. No, you just pick out a relative and bang away, and you are sure to get him. A youth who can't hit a cathedral at thirty yards with a Gatling gun in three quarters of an hour, can take up an old empty musket and bag his grandmother every time, at a hundred. Think what Waterloo would have been if one of the armies had been boys armed with old muskets supposed not to be loaded, and the other army had been composed of their female relations. The very thought of it makes one shudder.

There are many sorts of books ; but good ones are the sort for the young to read. Remember that. They are a great, an inestimable, and unspeakable means of improvement. Therefore be careful in your selection, my young friends ; be very careful ; confine yourselves exclusively to Robertson's *Sermons, Baxter's*

Saint's Rest, *The Innocents Abroad*, and works of that kind.

But I have said enough. I hope you will treasure the instructions which I have given you, and make them a guide to your feet and a light to your understanding. Build your character thoughtfully and **painstakingly** upon these precepts, and by and by, when you have got it built, you will be surprised and gratified to see how nicely and sharply it resembles everybody else's.

唐纳德

获悉人们希望我在这里讲几句时，我就问他们我该讲些什么。他们希望我讲些适合年轻人的东西——一些教诲性、有教育意义的东西，或是一些好的建议。这太好了！我倒是一直想给年轻人提点建议呢，因为人在年轻时期，好的建议极易在心底扎根，并能终生受用。那么，首先，年轻朋友们——我要真诚地告诫你们：

一定要听父母的话。长远来讲，这是最聪明的做法，如果你不听话，他们就会逼着你听话。大多数父母认为他们知道得比你们多，在这种情况下，与其基于自己的判断行事，还不如迎合他们的想法，这样你会收获更多。

如果你有上级的话，请尊重他们，对陌生人和他人也是如此。如果某个人得罪了你，而你也不知道他是否是故意的，那就不要采用极端做法，而要等待时机，给他当头一棒，这就够了；如果发现他并非有意伤害你，那么，你就应该站出来，坦白承认教训他的事；要像一个男子汉一样承认错误并说明自己并非有意。还有就是，切勿使用暴力。在这个和平友好的年代，暴力已经过时了。让我们谴责这些低俗的举止、粉碎暴力吧！

早睡早起——这是十分明智的。有些人主动起床，也有些人被迫起床。当然在百灵鸟的歌声中起床是最惬意不过的。当人人都知道你与百灵鸟同迎清晨，你便会备受称赞；如果你得到一只中意的百灵鸟，并按自己的意愿训练它，让他九点半，甚至是任何时候起床都不是件难事——当然，这并不是说要要诡计。

现在，我们来谈谈说谎吧。要说谎，就得小心谨慎，否则很容易穿帮。一旦被揭穿，别人就不再认为你是善良的和纯洁的，他们眼中的你就不是从前的你了。很多年轻人就因为一个笨拙或并不圆满的谎言永远地伤害了自己，原因在于他们不够谨慎且缺乏训练。有些人认为，年轻人不能撒谎。当然，这有些偏激。我不会这么偏激，而是始终相信自己是有道理的，我认为，年轻人应适当运用这门伟大的艺术，通过训练和实践，他们将变得自信、优雅和精确，而这些恰恰可以使他们完美出色地完成任务。耐心、勤奋和对细节的认真揣摩——都是年轻人必须具备的条件。随着时间的流逝，这些要素将会使你们臻于完美，而你们也只有仰仗这些要素才能成就日后的辉煌。想想那位无可匹敌的大师吧，多年沉闷乏味的学习、思考、实践和练习才使得他得以在世人面前说出这样的经典语句——"真理有着巨大的力量，并将战胜一切"——这是最伟大的悖论，是凡人所能达到的最高境界。历史和个人的经历都深刻地表明：真理易被推翻，但绝妙的谎言却永远颠扑不破。波士顿立有一座纪念麻醉术发明者的纪念碑。但后来，很多人发现，这个人根本不是麻醉术的发明者，他不过是窃取了他人的成果。真理的力量真的很强大吗？它能战胜一切吗？哦，不，朋友们，那座纪念碑是用很坚固的材料做成，但它所昭示的谎言将比纪念碑本身还要久一百万年。笨拙、没有说服力和漏洞百出的谎言是你应当通过不断学习去避免的，这样的谎言还不及一般真理长久。为什么呢，你还是说出真相吧，现在就说。一个没有说服力、可笑、荒谬的谎言不会存在两年——除非它是对某人的诽谤。当然，这样的谎言牢不可破，但这对你的名誉没有什么好处。一句话：尽早练习这门高尚而美丽的艺术吧——现在就开始。要是我当年入门早，现在就已经学会了。

切不要随便玩弄枪械。年轻人因为无知和不小心摆弄枪械而造成痛苦和伤害的例子太多了！就在 4 天前，我避暑的农舍隔壁住着一位满头银发、和蔼可亲的老奶奶，她是世界上最可亲的老人家之一了。当时，她正坐在那儿干活。她的小孙子蹑手蹑脚溜了进来，还拿着一管旧的、变了形的、锈迹斑斑的枪，这支枪好多年没用了，大家都以为里边没装子弹。孙子用枪指着她，笑着威胁她。她十分惊恐。惊叫着跑开了，并在门的另一侧求饶。但当她从他身边走过时，他用枪几乎顶着她的胸膛，并且扣动了板机！他以为枪膛里没子弹。的确是——枪里确实没子弹，所以并没有造成什么伤害。这是我听过的唯一一桩例外。因此，同样地，不要去碰没有装子弹的枪。它们是人类制造出的最精确的夺命工具。不要在枪支上浪费精力，不要给枪装支架，不要装瞄准器，甚至不要去瞄准。不，你只要拿起一样类似的东西并且"砰砰"两下，保证你会击中目标。一个在 45 分钟之内无法用加特林击中 30 码远的教堂的年轻人，可能会用一支破旧的没装子弹的枪在一百码处次次击中他的奶奶。想想看，如果滑铁卢战役中的一方是拿着没装子弹的枪的孩子们，另一方是他们的女性亲戚，结果会如何呢？只要想想，就会让人不寒而栗。

书有各种各样的，但好书才适合年轻人阅读。请记住，好书能让你不断完善自身，这种作用力强大，不可估量且难以名状。因此，年轻的朋友们，请谨慎选择你们的读物，要十分谨慎。你们应该专门读罗伯逊的《道德启示录》、巴克斯特的《圣徒的安息》和《傻瓜出国记》等作品。

我说得已经够多了。我希望你们能珍惜这些建议，让它们成为你的向导，点燃你们思想的火花。按照这些建议去努力培养自己的性格吧。慢慢地，一旦你塑造好了自己的性格，你将惊喜而欣慰地发现，自己和他人是如此相似。

Practising

核心单词

didactic [di'dæktik(əl)] *adj.* 为教导的；教训的

beseechingly [bi'si:tʃiŋli] *adv.* 恳求地；乞求地

dynamite ['dainəmait] *n.* 炸药　*v.* 用炸药爆破；炸毁

splendid ['splendid] *adj.* 灿烂的；壮丽的；辉煌的

permanently ['pɜ:məntli] *adv.* 永久地；长期不变地

tedious ['ti:diəs] *adj.* 冗长乏味的；使人厌烦的

majestic [mə'dʒestik] *adj.* 雄伟的；威严的；崇高的

fright [frait] *n.* 惊吓，恐怖

painstakingly ['peins,teikiŋli] *adv.* 刻苦地；煞费苦心地

实用句型

Go to bed early, get up early—this is wise. 早睡早起——这是十分明智的。

①这是祈使句＋简单句的句型。

② Go to bed early, get up early 早睡早起，类似的谚语还有 An idle youth, a needy age. 少壮不努力，老大徒伤悲；Everything has its time and that time must be watched. 万物皆有时，时来不可失；Practice makes perfect. 熟能生巧等。

翻译行不行

1. 明天应该是个好天气。(ought to)

....

2. 拿不准词义时就查查词典。(in doubt)

....

3. 很容易从人群中辨认出他，因为他个子很高。(pick out)

....

Life Is the Cookie
生命就是小甜饼

· Martha Russell ·

One of my patients, a successful businessman, tells me that before his cancer he would become depressed unless things went a certain way. Happiness was "having the cookie."

If you had the cookie, things were good. If you didn't have the cookie, life wasn't worth a damn. Unfortunately, the cookie kept changing. Some of the time it was money, sometimes power, sometimes sex. At other times, it was the new car, the biggest contract, the most **prestigious** address.

A year and a half after his **diagnosis** of prostate cancer he sits shaking his head **ruefully**.

"It's like I stopped learning how to live after I was a kid. When I give my son a cookie, he is happy. If I take the cookie away or it breaks, he is unhappy. But he is two and a half and I am forty-three. It's taken me this long to understand that the cookie will never make me happy for long.

"The minute you have the cookie it starts to crumble or you start to worry about it **crumbling** or about someone trying to take it away from you. You know, you have to give up a lot of things to take care of the cookie, to keep it from crumbling and be sure that no one takes it away from you. You may not even get a chance to eat it because you are so busy just trying not to lose it. Having the cookie is not what life is about."

My patient laughs and says cancer has changed him. For the first time he is happy. No matter if his business is doing well or not, no matter if he wins or loses at golf.

"Two years ago, cancer asked me, 'Okay, what's important? What is really important?' Well, life is important. Life. Life any way you can have it, life with the cookie, life without the cookie. Happiness does not have anything to do with the cookie; it has to do with being **alive**. Before, who made the time?" He pauses **thoughtfully**. "Damn, I guess life is the cookie."

生活就像一盒巧克力

玛莎·鲁塞尔

我的一位病人，是一位成功的商人。他告诉我，在他患癌症之前，凡事如果没有确定下来，他就会忧心忡忡。对他而言，幸福是"拥有小甜饼"。

如果你拥有了小甜饼，一切都一帆风顺。如果你没有小甜饼，生活就一文不值。不幸的是，小甜饼总是在不断地变换着，有时是金钱，有时是权力，有时是欲望。而有的时候，它又是一辆新车、一份数额庞大的合同，或是一个享有声望的通讯地址。

在他被诊断出患有前列腺癌的一年半之后，他坐在那里，悲天悯人地摇着头，说："长大以后，我好像就不知道该怎样生活了。当我给我儿子一个小甜饼时，他心花怒放。如果我拿走甜饼或者是小甜饼碎了，他就闷闷不乐。不同的是，他只有两岁半，而我已经43岁了。我花了这么长的时间才明白小甜饼并不能使我长久的感到幸福。

"从你拥有小甜饼的那一刻，它就开始破碎，或者你就开始担心它会破碎，抑或你开始担心别人会拿走它。为了守护你的小甜饼，为了防止它破碎或者确定别人不会从你手中夺走它，你不得不放弃许多东西。你忙于不让自己失去它，甚至没有时间享受它。拥有小甜饼并不是生活的全部内容。"

我的病人笑着说癌症已经改变了他。不论他的生意是否顺利，不论他在打高尔夫球时是输是赢，他有生以来第一次感到幸福。

"两年前，癌症问我'什么重要？什么是真正重要的？'对，生命重要。生命。生命，无论如何你拥有生命。有小甜饼也罢，没有小甜饼也罢，幸福与小甜饼并非息息相关，而是与生命的存在有关。可是，时光一去不复返，谁又能让时光倒流呢？"他停顿了一下，若有所思，说："该死的，我觉得生命就是那块小甜饼"。

核心单词

prestigious [ˌpres'tidʒəs] *adj.* 有名望的

diagnosis [ˌdaiəg'nəusis] *n.* 诊断；诊断结果

ruefully ['ru:ʃəli] *adv.* 悲伤地；可怜地；悲惨地

crumble ['krʌmbl] *v.* 粉碎，弄碎；破坏

alive [ə'laiv] *adj.* 活着的；现存的；活跃的

thoughtfully ['θɔ:tʃəli] *adv.* 沉思地；深虑地；考虑周到地

实用句型

If you had the cookie, things were good.

如果你拥有了小甜饼，一切都一帆风顺。

①虚拟语气：if+had，表示跟现在事实相反的假设。

② things are good 一帆风顺，类似的表达还有 good luck 好运，good night 晚安等。

翻译行不行

1. 很多国家需要更先进的装置来处理工业废物。(take care of)

....

2. 他忍不住大笑。(keep from)

....

3. 你不必把此事告诉他。(have to)

....

Carrot，Egg or Coffee
胡萝卜，鸡蛋还是咖啡豆

A daughter complained to her father about her life and how things were so hard for her. *She did not know how she was going to make it and wanted to give up*. She was tired of fighting and struggling. It seemed as one problem was solved a new one arose.

Her father, a cook, took her to the kitchen. He filled three pots with water and placed each on a high fire. Soon the pots came to a boil. In one he placed carrots, in the second he placed eggs，and in the last he placed ground coffee beans. He let them sit and boil，without saying a word.

The daughter sucked her teeth and **impatiently** waited, wondering what he was doing. In about twenty minutes he turned off the burners. He fished the carrots out and placed them in a bowl. He pulled the eggs out and placed them a bowl. Then he ladled the coffee out and placed it in a mug. Turning to her he asked, "Darling, what do you see?"

"Carrots，eggs, and coffee," she replied.

He brought her closer and asked her to feel the carrots. She did and noted that they were soft. He then asked her to take an egg and break it. After pulling off the shell, she observed the hard-boiled egg. Finally, he asked her to sip the coffee. She smiled, as she tasted its rich aroma.

"What does it mean, Father?" She **humbly** asked.

He explained that each of them had faced the same **adversity**, boiling water, but each reacted differently. The carrot went in strong, hard, and **unrelenting**. But after being subjected to the boiling water, it softened and became weak. The egg had been fragile. Its thin outer shell had protected its liquid **interior**. But after sitting through the boiling water, its inside became hardened. The ground coffee beans were unique, however. After they were in the boiling water, they had changed the water.

"Which are you?" he asked his daughter.

When adversity knocks on your door, how do you respond? Are you a carrot, an egg, or a coffee bean?

117

杰罗姆

女儿向父亲抱怨她的生活，她觉得凡事都很艰难，不知该怎样面对，想要放弃。她厌倦了不断地抗争和奋斗，好像一个问题刚刚解决，另一个又出现了。

她的父亲是名厨师，他把她带进了厨房，在三个壶里分别装了水，然后放到火上烧。很快，壶里的水开了。他往第一个壶里放了些胡萝卜、往第二个里放了鸡蛋，在最后一个里放了些磨碎的咖啡豆，然后静静地等着它们煮沸。

女儿噘着嘴，不耐烦地等着，对父亲的行为感到很纳闷。大约20分钟后，父亲关了火炉，把胡萝卜捞出来，放在一个碗里，又把鸡蛋拿出来放进另一个碗里，接着把咖啡倒进了一个杯子里，然后转过头来，对她说，“亲爱的，你看见了什么？”

“胡萝卜、鸡蛋和咖啡，”她答道。

父亲拉近她并让她去摸胡萝卜，她摸了摸，觉得它们变柔软了。然后，他又让她去把鸡蛋敲破，把蛋壳剥掉后，她看到了一个熟鸡蛋。最后，父亲要她喝咖啡。在尝过芳香四溢的咖啡后。她笑了。

“这是什么意思，父亲？”她谦恭地问道。

父亲解释说，这三样东西面临着同样的逆境——煮沸的水，但它们的反应却各不相同。胡萝卜本是强硬，坚固而不甘示弱的。但受到开水的影响后，它变得柔软而脆弱。鸡蛋本来易碎，薄薄的外壳保护着内部的液体。但用开水煮过以后，它的内部就变得坚硬。不过，最独特的是磨碎的咖啡豆。经过沸腾的水后，它们却改变了水。

“哪一个是你呢？”他问女儿。

当不幸降临到你头上时，你该如何应对呢？你是胡萝卜、鸡蛋，还是咖啡豆？

Practising

& Exercise

核心单词

impatiently [im'peiʃəntli] *adv.* 不耐烦地；性急地

humbly [hʌmbli] *adv.* 谦逊地，恭顺地

adversity [əd'və:siti] *n.* 逆境；厄运；不幸的事

unrelenting ['ʌnri'lentiŋ] *adj.* 不宽恕的；无情的；坚定的

interior [in'tiəriə] *adj.* 内的，内部的

实用句型

She did not know how she was going to make it and wanted to give up.

她不知该怎样面对，想要放弃。

①这里是由 how 引导的宾语从句。

② make 后用不带 to 的不定式，类似的词还有 have, let, help, suggest 等。

翻译行不行

1. 离开前请关灯。(turn off)

....

2. 他脱下大衣，开始工作。(pull off)

....

3. 这受市场需求的影响。(be subject to)

....

Our Kind Landlord
我们的好房东

· Sammy ·

Two friends and I moved into a house off **campus** when I was a **junior** at Iowa State University. We were all a bit afraid of our landlord, a gruff middle-aged man. He gave us a lecture about paying the rent on time and maintaining the house and **appliances**.

During the fall semester, my housemates and I threw a party. We sent invitations to many friends and told everyone to come to our house on Friday night. We drew a large crowd and everyone had a great time. The last guests left in the wee hours of the morning.

Exhausted, we decided to sleep in and clean the house and yard the next morning. Well, you guessed it! We were awakened about 7:00 a.m. by our landlord, who was knocking on the door. Sheepishly, we let him in, expecting to incur his wrath. Instead, he picked up a party invitation that had been laying on the sidewalk and asked, "Why didn't you girls invite me?" He came into the house, made a minor repair, and spent a few minutes helping us pick up trash from the yard. We weren't quite sure what to make of our unexpected luck, but we were thrilled that our landlord had been so understanding.

A few months later, I made a mathematical error while balancing my checkbook and my bank soon notified me that I had bounced a check. I was mortified when I discovered that it was my rent check and that I had to **notify** my landlord, I figured that he viewed my housemates and I as irresponsible after the party incident and this would prove him right. I was certain that he would **evict** me. Somehow, I mustered the courage to call him and explained what had happened. He said, "I have a daughter about your age, and the same thing happened to her once. *Would you like to wait until next month and send a double payment then?*"

I've never forgotten our landlord's kindness and understanding. He also taught me an important lesson about not judging a book by its cover. I'm proud to say that I have not bounced a check since (though I have thrown a few more parties)!

萨 米

在爱荷华州立大学读大三时，我和两个朋友从宿舍搬出来，租了一间房子。房东是一个粗鲁的中年人，我们都有点怕他。

他交代我们要及时交房租，保护好房子和电器。

下半学期，我和室友举办了一个聚会。我们邀请了许多朋友，让他们星期五晚上都到家里来玩。我们一大群人玩得很尽兴，最后一个客人在天快要亮时才离开。

我们玩得筋疲力尽，决定先睡觉，第二天早上起来再清扫房子。噢，你猜怎么着。早上七点时，我们被房东的敲门声吵醒，我们不好意思地让他进来，料想会遭他怒骂。谁知，他拣起过道边的一张宴会请柬，问道："你们这些女孩子怎么不邀请我呢，"他走进屋子，简单清理了一下，又帮我们把院子的垃圾清扫了。我们也不知道怎么这么走运，兴奋地发现我们的房东竟如此通情达理。

数月后，由于我计算失误，账户上没有余额了。银行很快给我发了退票。我羞愧地发现那是我给房东的月租支票，而我又不得不告诉房东。那次聚会后，我想他一定以为我和室友们都是不负责任的人，现在更证实了他的看法。我想他一定会把我们赶出去的。可不知为什么，当我鼓起勇气给他打电话解释时，他说，"我有一个女儿跟你们差不多大。她曾经也干过相同的事。你不想等到下个月给我双份月租吗？"

我永远都忘不了房东的善心和通情达理。他教给我一个重要的人生道理：切勿以貌取人。我自豪地说，从那以后我再也没收到银行的退票（尽管我又举办过几次聚会）。

核心单词

campus ['kæmpəs] *n.* 校园，校区

junior ['dʒuːnjə] *adj.* 年纪较轻的；三年级（生）的

appliance [ə'plaiəns] *n.* 器具；装置，设备

notify ['nəutifai] *v.* 通知，告知；报告

evict [i(ː)'vikt] *v.* （房客等）逐出；收回（财产等）

实用句型

Would you like to wait until next month and send a double payment then?

你不想等到下个月给我双份月租吧？

① Would you like to...?"要不要……?"表示邀请或提出建议。这是一种很有礼貌的表达。

② double payment 双份月租，类似的表达还有 double pay 双倍工钱；a double room 双人房；a double significance 双重意义；double tongue 两面派，表里不一等固定搭配。

翻译行不行

1. 请你把收音机声音关小一点好吗？(a bit)

....

2. 你昨晚在晚会上玩得开心吗？(have a great time)

....

3. 我们两人的想法不谋而合。(happen to)

....

Life Throws a Brick at Your Head
生活中的 "砖头"

• Ralph Mondy •

A young and successful **executive** was traveling down a neighborhood street, going a bit too fast in his new Jaguar. He was watching for kids darting out from between parked cars and slowed down when he thought he saw something.

As his car passed, one child appeared, and a brick smashed into the Jag's side door. He slammed on the brakes and spun the Jag back to the **spot** from where the brick had been thrown.

He jumped out of the car, grabbed some kid and pushed him up against a parked car, shouting, "What was that all about and who are you? Just what the heck are you doing?" Building up a head of steam, he went on, "That's a new car and that brick you threw is going to cost a lot of money. Why did you do it?"

"Please, mister, please, I'm sorry. I didn't know what else to do!" **pleaded** the youngster.

"It's my brother," he said, "He rolled off the curb and fell out of his wheelchair and I can't lift him up. Sobbing, the boy asked the executive, "*Would you please help me get him back into his wheelchair?*" He's hurt and he's too heavy for me."

Moved beyond words, the driver tried to **swallow** the rapidly swelling lump in his throat. He lifted the young man back into the wheelchair and took out his handkerchief and wiped the scrapes and cuts, **checking** to see that everything was going to be okay.

"Thank you, sir. And God bless you," the grateful child said to him. The man then watched the little boy push his brother to the sidewalk toward their home.

It was a long walk back to his Jaguar... a long, slow walk. He never did repair to the side door. He kept the dent to remind him not to go through life so fast that someone has to throw a brick at you to get your attention.

Life whispers in your soul and speaks to your heart. Sometimes, when you have no time to listen... it's your choice: Listen to the **whispers** of your soul or wait for the brick!

拉尔夫·穆迪

一位年轻的总裁，开着他的新捷豹车快速经过住宅区的巷道。他也一直提防着那些从停放的车子中间突然蹿出来的孩子，他想只要一有情况，就立即减速。

就在他的车经过时一个小朋友出来并丢了一块砖头打到了他的车门，他很生气地踩了刹车并后退到砖头丢出来的地方。

他跳出车外，抓住了那个小孩，把他顶在车门上说："你为什么这样做，你知道你刚刚做了什么吗？"接着又吼道："你知道要赔多少钱来修理这辆新车，你到底为什么要这样做？"

小孩子央求着说："先生，对不起，我不知道我该怎么办？"

他接着说："因为我哥哥从轮椅上掉了下来，我没办法把他抬回去。"他啜泣着问道："你可以帮我把他抬回去吗？他受伤了，可是他太重了我抱不动。"

听了这些话，年轻的总裁深受感动，他抱起男孩受伤的哥哥，把他放回到轮椅上，拿出手帕擦拭他哥哥的伤口，并细心察看有没有什么大问题。

小男孩感激地说："谢谢你，先生，上帝会保佑你的。"然后男孩推着他哥哥朝家的方向走去。

年轻总裁回到捷豹车的路变得如此的漫长，他也没有修汽车的车门。他保留着车上的凹痕就是为了提醒自己：生活的道路不要走得太匆忙，否则就需要其他人的敲打来让自己注意生活的真谛。

当生命想与你的心灵窃窃私语时，你若没有时间，你可以有两种选择：倾听你心灵的声音或者让砖头来砸你！

Practising
& Exercise

实战
提升篇

核心单词

executive [igˈzekjutiv] *adj.* 执行的；实施的；经营管理的

spot [spɒt] *n.* 斑点，斑块；污点

plead [pliːd] *v.* 辩护，抗辩

swallow [ˈswɔləu] *v.* 吞下，咽下

check [tʃek] *n.* 检查，核对

whisper [ˈ(h)wispə] *v.* 低语，耳语

实用句型

Would you please help me get him back into his wheelchair?

你可以帮我把他抬回去吗？

① would 在这里表示委婉的建议或请求，"请……好吗？"。

② get back 恢复，取回，类似的表达还有 get from 从……取得；get out of 取出；get away 逃脱等固定搭配。

翻译行不行

1. 前方学校，慢行！（slow down）

....

2. 他听到这个消息后，从床上一跃而起。（jump out of）

....

3. 新法案未能通过。（go through）

....

There Are No Mistakes, Only Lessons
没有错误，只有教训

Human growth is a process of experimentation, trial, and error, ultimately leading to wisdom. Each time you choose to trust yourself and take action, you can never quite be certain how the situation will turn out. Sometimes you are victorious, and sometimes you become disillusioned. The failed experiments, however, are no less valuable than the experiments that ultimately prove successful; in fact, you usually learn more from your perceived "failures" than you do from your perceived "successes".

If you have made what you perceive to be a mistake, or failed to live up to your own expectations, you will most likely put up a barrier between your essence and the part of you that is the **alleged** wrong-doer. However, perceiving past actions as mistakes implies guilt and blame, and it is not possible to learn anything meaningful while you are engaged in blaming. *Therefore, forgiveness is required when you are harshly judging yourself.*

Forgiveness is the act of erasing an emotional debt. There are four kinds of forgiveness:

The first is beginner forgiveness for yourself.

The second kind of forgiveness is beginner forgiveness for another.

The third kind of forgiveness is advanced forgiveness of yourself. This is for serious transgressions, the ones you carry with deep shame. When you do something that violates your own values and **ethics**, you create a chasm between your standards and your actual behavior. In such a case, you need to work very hard at forgiving yourself for these deeds so that you can close this chasm and realign with the best part of yourself. This does not mean that you should rush to forgive yourself or not feel regret or remorse ; but **wallowing** in these feelings for a protracted period of time is not healthy, and punishing yourself excessively will only create a bigger gap between you and your ethics.

The last and perhaps most difficult one is the advanced forgiveness of another. At some time of our life, you may have been **severely** wronged or hurt by another person to such a degree that forgiveness seems impossible. However, harboring resentment and revenge **fantasies** only keeps you trapped in victimhood. Under such a circumstance, you should force yourself to see the bigger picture, by so doing, you will be able to shift the focus away from the anger and resentment. It is only through forgiveness that you can erase **wrongdoing** and clean the memory. When you can finally release the situation, you may come to see it as a necessary part of your growth.

里 奇

　　人的成长是一个不断尝试、不断经历失误、又不断获得新知的过程。每次，当你信心十足并准备采取行动时，对于会有什么样的结果，你无从知晓——或许成功，或许失败。然而，失败并不意味着毫无价值。事实上，我们往往能从失败中学到比成功中更多的东西。

　　假如你犯了一个错误，或是未达到自己所期望的标准，你很可能会在真我与所谓的犯错者之间构筑一道壁垒。然而，对以往的行为全盘否定，势必会让你感到内疚、自责。当你深陷其中时，就不可能从中汲取到有益的东西。因此，过分苛求自己时，最需要的就是自我宽恕。

　　宽恕就是放下情感上的包袱，抹平心灵上的创伤。它有四种类型：

　　第一种是对自己的初级宽恕。

　　第二种是对他人的初级宽恕。

　　第三种是对自己更深层次的宽恕。这种宽恕是针对自己深感羞愧的极大恶行而言。如果你所做的事有悖于自己的价值观和道德观，这时，你就在自己的为人准则和实际行动间制造了一道裂痕。在这种情况下，你就必须努力悔改，以此来弥补过错，并要重新找到自我。当然，这并不是说你可以随意地原谅自己，毫无悔改之意，但一味地埋怨自己是不健康的，过分的自我惩罚只会让你偏离自己道德准则的轨道越来越远。

　　第四种可能是最难的一种宽恕——是对他人深层次的宽恕。生活中，你也许会受到极大的委屈和伤害，以此来看，这似乎是不可原谅的。但是，心怀怨恨、企图报复只会使你陷于受伤害的阴影中。在这种情况下，你就要强迫自己放宽胸怀。只有这样，你才能把注意力从恼怒和仇恨中转移开来。只有做到宽恕，你才能忘却过错，净化心灵。于是，当你最终把自己解脱出来时，很自然地，你就会把它看成是成长过程中必不可少的一部分。

核心单词

allege [əˈledʒ] *v.* 断言，宣称

ethics [ˈeθiks] *n.* 伦理观，道德标准

wallow [ˈwɔləu] *v.* 沉迷；纵乐

severely [siˈviəli] *adv.* 严格地；严厉地；严重地

fantasy [ˈfæntəsi] *n.* 空想；幻想；梦想

wrongdoing [ˈrɔŋˈduːiŋ] *n.* 做坏事；犯罪

实用句型

Therefore, forgiveness is required when you are harshly judging yourself. 因此，过分苛求自己时，最需要的就是自我宽恕。

① is required 是一般现在时的被动语态，基本形式为 is\am\are+P.P（过去分词）。

② forgiveness 宽恕，饶恕，名词后缀 ness 加在形容词后构成抽象名词，类似的例子还有 kindess 仁慈；tiredness 疲劳；happiness 幸福，快乐，愉快；sadness 悲哀，悲伤等。

翻译行不行

1. 他的身份不亚于部长。(no less than)

....

2. 他没有实行他宣布的原则。(live up to)

....

3. 不要开小差，集中精力。(shift away from)

....

The Cobbler and the Banker
皮匠和银行家

• La Fontaine •

A cobbler passed his time in singing from morning till night ; it was wonderful to see, wonderful to hear him ; he was more contented in making shoes than was any of the seven sages. His neighbor, on the contrary, who was rolling in wealth, sung but little, and sleepless. He was a banker ; when by chance he fell into a doze at day-break, the cobbler awoke him with his song. The banker **complained** sadly that Providence had not made sleep a saleable commodity, like edibles or drinkables. Having at length sent for the songster, he said to him, "How much a year do you earn, Master Gregory?"

"How much a year, sir?" said the merry cobbler laughing, "I never **reckon** in that way, living as I do from one day to another ; somehow I manage to reach the end of the year ; each day brings its meal."

"Well then! How much a day do you earn, my friend?"

"Sometimes more, sometimes less ; but the worst of it is, and, without that our earnings would be very **tolerable**, a number of days occur in the year on which we are forbidden to work ; and the curate, moreover, is constantly adding some new saint to the list."

The banker, laughing at his simplicity, said, "In the future I shall place you above want. Take this hundred crowns, preserve them carefully, and make use of them in time of need."

The cobbler fancied he beheld all the wealth which the earth had produced in the past century for the use of mankind. Returning home, he buried his money and his happiness at the same time. No more singing; he lost his voice, the moment he acquired that which is the source of so much grief. Sleep quitted his dwelling; and cares, **suspicions**, and false alarms took its place. All day, his eye wandered in the direction of the treasure; and at night, if some **stray** cat made a noise, the cat was robbing him. At length the poor man ran to the house of his rich neighbor; "Give me back," said he, "sleep and my voice, and take your hundred crowns."

拉·封丹

　　一个皮匠以歌自娱,在歌声中度过每一天。每一个见到他,或听到他歌声的人都甚感愉快。他安于自己的制鞋工作,甚至觉得比当希腊七圣还感满足。他的邻居是一个家财万贯的银行家,与他相反,银行家很少唱歌,睡眠也不好,偶尔在天快亮时才打个盹，又被皮匠的歌声吵醒了。他痛苦地抱怨上帝没把睡眠也变成商品，他多想睡眠也像食品和饮料那样能随意购买啊。最后，银行家把这个歌唱者请了过来，对他说："格雷戈里师傅，您一年能赚多少钱啊？"

"一年赚多少钱吗，先生？"快乐的皮匠笑道，"我可从来没有这样统计过，我天天这么过着，每天挣足三餐，总能撑到年底。"

"啊，朋友，那么，你一天挣多少呢？"

"有时候挣得多，有时又少点，我们的收入还可以。最难过的日子就是每年总有些时候不让我们工作，而牧师又常吸纳新的圣徒。"

银行家被皮匠的直率逗乐了，他说，"今后，我将满足你的一切需求，你把这一百枚钱拿去存好，需要时就拿出来用。"

皮匠觉得自己好像看到了几个世纪以来，大地为人类所需而创造出来的所有财富。他回家后，把这笔钱给埋了起来，同时，也埋葬了他的欢乐。从此，他不再唱歌。在他得到钱这个痛苦根源的那刻起，就失去了歌喉。担心、怀疑、虚惊让他不能安稳入睡。他的目光整天游移在藏钱的地方。晚上，就是野猫弄出点声响，他也会以为是有人来抢他的宝贝。最后，这个可怜的人跑到他富有的邻居那里，"还我睡眠和歌喉吧，把你的一百枚钱币拿回去。"

核心单词

complain [kəm'plein] v. 抱怨，发牢骚；投诉

reckon ['rekən] v. 测算，测量；认为

tolerable ['tɔlərəbl] adj. 可容忍的；可宽恕的

suspicious [səs'piʃəs] adj. 猜疑的，疑心的；多疑的

stray [strei] v. 迷路，走失；走散

实用句型

The banker, laughing at his simplicity, said, "In the future I shall place you above want".

银行家被皮匠的直率逗乐了，他说，"今后，我将满足你的一切需求"。

① laughing at his simplicity 在这里是插入语，如果将其删掉，句子结构仍然完整。

② in the future 将来，类似的表达还有 in the days to come；in the coming days 等固定搭配。

翻译行不行

1. 相反，这是符合爱好和平的人们的利益的。(on the contrary)

....

2. 我完全是侥幸打赢的。(by chance)

....

3. 他对他的工作进行了详细的阐述。(at length)

....

伙，掉过头来对着我们破口大骂。我的司机只是微笑着，冲他挥挥手。我只想说，他那表现相当的友好！

所以，我问他："你干嘛那样？那家伙差点撞毁你的车，还差点让我们都进医院！"

然后这个司机给我讲了我现在称之为"垃圾车法则"的道理。

"许多人像垃圾车。他们满载着垃圾四处转悠，满载着挫败、愤怒和失望。他们的垃圾堆得像小山那么高，他们得找个地方倾倒，所以如果你由着他们，他们就把垃圾倒在你身上。当有人想往你身上倒垃圾的时候，你别往心里去。相反，就冲他们笑笑并挥挥手好了，祝愿他们好运，然后继续走你的路。你如果这么做了，会比较开心。"

哇噢，这还真的让我思索起来，有多少次我由得垃圾车向我驶来，而且，有多少次我忍受了他们的垃圾，并且再倒给别的人：同事、家人、路人。就是在那天我下定了决心，"我再也不这样做了。"

从那时起，我到处都看得见垃圾车。就好像电影《第六感》中的孩子说"我看见死人"那样，如今我说："我看见垃圾车。"

我看见他们满载着那些东西……我看见他们打算卸下来。正像我的出租车司机那样，我不往心里去；我只是微笑，挥手，祝他们好运，然后我该干吗还干吗。

Practising

& Exercise

核心单词

lesson ['lesn] *n.* 功课；课业；教训

mere [miə] *adj.* 仅仅的，只不过的

frustration [frʌs'treiʃən] *n.* 挫折，失败，挫败

spread [spred] *v.* 使伸展，使延伸

personal ['pəːsənl] *adj.* 个人的，私人的

实用句型

It was that day I resolved，"I'm not going to do it anymore."

就是在那天我下定了决心，"我再也不这样做了"。

①这是一个强调句。

② anymore 和 any more 都表示"再也"。两者皆可用在句子结尾，但在作定语时只能用 any more 而不能用 anymore。

翻译行不行

1. 飞机马上就要起飞了。(take off)

....

2. 我们的工作越积越多了。(pile up)

....

3. 这家公司的生意日益清淡。(drop off)

....

Get a Thorough Understanding of Oneself
彻悟自我，善待自我

· Anonymous ·

In all one's lifetime it is oneself that one spends the most time being with or dealing with. *But it is precisely oneself that one has the least understanding of.*

When you are going upwards in life you tend to overestimate yourself. When you are going **downhill** you tend to underestimate yourself.

It's likely that you think it wise for yourself to know your place and stay **aloof** from worldly events wearing a mask of cowardice, behind which the flow of sap in your life will be **retarded**.

To get a thorough understanding of oneself is to gain a correct view of oneself and be a **sober** realist—aware of both one's strength and shortage.

You may look forward hopefully to the future but be sure not to expect too much, for ideals can never be fully realized.

You may be courageous to meet challenges but it should be clear to you where to direct your efforts.

To get a thorough understanding of oneself needs self-appreciation.

Whether you liken yourself to a towering tree or a blade of grass, whether you think you are a high mountain or a small stone, you represent a state of nature that has its own reason of existence.

If you earnestly admire yourself you'll have a real sense of self-appreciation, which will give you confidence.

As soon as you gain full confidence in yourself you'll be enabled to fight and overcome any **adversity**.

To get a thorough understanding of oneself also requires doing oneself a favor when it's needed.

In time of anger, do yourself a favor by giving vent to it in a quiet place so that you won't be hurt by its flames ; in time of sadness, do yourself a favor by sharing it with your friends so as to change a **gloomy** mood into a cheerful one ; in time of tiredness, do yourself a favor by getting a good sleep or taking some tonic. Show yourself loving concern about your health and daily life.

Unless you know perfectly well when and how to do yourself a favor, you won't be confident and ready enough to **resist** the attack of illness.

To get a thorough understanding of oneself is to get a full control of one's life. Then one will find one's life full of color and flavor.

人生在世，和自己相处最多，打交道最多，但是最不了解的也恰恰是自己。

当你一帆风顺时，往往高估自己；不得志时，又往往低估自己。

你可能认为安分守己、与世无争是明智之举，而实际上往往被怯懦的面具窒息了自己鲜活的生命。

彻悟自己，就是要正确认识自己，做一个冷静的现实主义者，既清楚自己的优势，也知道自己的不足。

我们可以憧憬人生，但不要期望过高。因为在现实中，理想的实现总是会打折扣的。

你可以勇敢地迎接挑战，但是必须清楚自己努力的方向。

要彻悟自己就要欣赏自己。

无论你是一棵参天大树，还是一棵无名小草，无论你认为自己是一座高山，还是一块石头，你都是一种天然，都有自己存在的理由。

只要你认真地欣赏自己，你就会拥有一个真正的自我，你才会拥有信心。

一旦拥有了信心你就能战胜任何灾难。

要彻悟自己，就要善待自己。

在气愤时，善待自己，找个僻静之处宣泄一下，不要被那些无名之火伤身；忧伤时，要善待自己，找个好友倾诉一番，让低迷的情绪高涨起来；劳累时，要善待自己，睡个好觉或者吃点滋补品，对自己的健康和生活关心备至。

　　唯有知道如何善待自己，你才会信心百倍，从容不迫地准备应对疾病的侵袭。

　　彻悟了自己，你才能把握自己的生命，你的生活才会丰富多彩、有滋有味！

核心单词

downhill ['daunhil] *adv.* 向下；向坡下；每况愈下

aloof [ə'lu:f] *adv.* 分开地；避开地

retarded [ri'tɑ:did] *adj.* 智力迟钝的，弱智的

sober ['səubə] *adj.* 认真的；严肃的，持重的

adversity [əd'və:siti] *n.* 逆境；灾祸；灾难；不幸的事

gloomy ['glu:mi] *adj.* 阴暗的；阴沉的；忧郁的

resist [ri'zist] *v.* 抵抗，反抗；抗拒

实用句型

But it is precisely oneself that one has the least understanding of.

但是人最不了解的也恰恰是自己。

① It is...that 结构强调 oneself。

② the least 最小，最少 (little 的最高级)，类似的还有 the worse 最差 (bad 的比较级)；the best 最好 (good 和 well 的最高级) 等。

翻译行不行

1. 现代家具的设计越来越简单了。(tend to)

....

2. 他们在期待着她的来访。(look forward to)

....

3. 对生态学的关心是近来的事。(concern about)

....

Alone but not Lonely
享受独处

It scares us more than anything except death being alone.

Our fear of aloneness is so ingrained that given the choice of being by ourselves or being with others we opt for safety in numbers, even at the expense of lingering in painful, boring, or totally unredeeming company.

And yet more of us than ever are alone.

While many Americans have their **solo** lifestyles thrust on them—people die, people go away—a huge and growing population is choosing to be alone.

In 1955, one in ten U.S. households consisted of one person. By 1999, the proportion was one in three. Single men and women accounted for 38.9million of the nation's 110.5 million households. By 1999, single parents with children under the age of eighteen made up 27.3 percent of the nation's 70.9 million family households. Meanwhile, many more Americans are divorcing. In less than three decades, the number of divorced men and women has more than quadrupled—to a total of 18.3 million in 1996, compared to 4.3 million in 1970. Never before in

American history has living alone been the predominant lifestyle.

Nonetheless, we persist in the conviction that a solitary existence is the harshest penalty life can mete out. We loathe being alone—anytime, anywhere, for whatever reason. From childhood we're conditioned to accept that when alone we **instinctively** ache for company, that loners are outsiders yearning to get in rather than people who are content with their own company.

Alone, we squander life by rejecting its full potential and wasting its remaining promises. Alone, we accept that experiences unshared are barely worthwhile, that sunsets viewed singly are not as spectacular, that time spent apart is fallow and pointless .

And so we grow old believing we are nothing by ourselves, steadfastly shunning the opportunities for self-discovery and personal growth that solitude could bring us.

We have even **coined** a word for those who prefer to be by themselves: antisocial, as if they were enemies of society. They are viewed as friendless, suspect in a world that goes around in twos or more and is wary of solitary travelers.

People who need people are threatened by people who don't. The idea of seeking contentment alone is heretical, for society steadfastly decrees that our completeness lies in others. Instead, we cling to each other for solace, comfort, and safety.

Ironically, most of us crave more **intimacy** and companionship than we can bear. We begrudge ourselves, our spouses, and our partners sufficient physical and emotional breathing room, and then bemoan the suffocation of our relationships.

To point out these facts is not to suggest we should abandon all our close ties. Medical surveys show that the majority of elderly people who live alone, yet maintain frequent contact with relatives and friends, rate their physical and emotional well-being as "excellent". Just as an apple a day kept the doctor away when they were young, an **active** social calendar appears to serve the same purpose now.

But we need to befriend and enjoy ourselves as well.

We must relearn to be alone. Instead of planting our solitude with dream blossoms, we choke the space with continuous music and chatter to which we do not even listen. It is simply there to fill the **vacuum**. We can't stand the silence, because silence includes thinking. And if we thought, we would have to face ourselves.

Let us learn, then, from those in search of what they have not been able to find and hold: peace of mind, gentleness of heart, calmness of spirit, daily joy. Who have come to understand that to know and to love and to be of value to others, they first must know and love and value themselves; that to find their way in the world, they have to start by finding themselves.

肖 恩

除了死亡，我们最害怕的就是孤独。

我们如此害怕孤独。以至于让我们选择是独处还是跟别人一起时，我们会选择后者以寻求安全感。甚至不惜付出如此多的代价：长久的痛苦、烦闷，或完全无益的陪伴。

然而，现在，我们却感受到了从未感受过的强烈孤独。

当许多美国人开始单身生活时——因为身边的人去世或离开——一个日益增加的庞大人群开始选择独身。

1955 年，美国家庭中有十分之一的单亲家庭。到 1999 年，这个比例扩大到三分之一。在这个国家里，110 000 000 个家庭中单亲家庭占了 38 900 000。到 1999 年，带着一个 18 岁以下小孩的单亲家庭已经占到了这个国家 70 900 000 个家庭的 27.3%。同时，更多的美国人离婚了。不到 30 年之间，离婚的人数增加为原来的 4 倍——到 1996 年这一数字已经达到 18 300 000，而 1970 年只有 4 300 000 人。独居史无前例地成为美国主流的生活方式。

然而，我们坚持认为，独居是最残酷的生活方式。我们讨厌独处——无论何时何地，出于何种原因。我们从孩提时候起就习惯认同，独处时的我们会本能地渴望有人陪伴，认为孤独者都是渴望加入群体生活，而非欣然独处的。

独处时，我们是在拒绝生命丰富多彩的可能，并耗费生命存留的希望，是在浪费生命。我们认为，无人分享的经历毫无价值，一个人看到的日出并非那么壮观，一个人度过的时光是多么了无生趣和毫无意义。

于是，当我们年老时，就认为自己无关紧要而倔强地逃避。殊不知这正是我们发现自我和个人成长的机会。

对于那些宁愿独居的人，我们甚至给他们扣上"反社会"的头衔，好像他们是社会的公敌，他们被人们认为是缺少朋友、怀疑这个世界的人。那些结伴同行者警惕地盯着这些孤独的旅行者。

依赖于他人的人受到独立的人的威胁，独自寻求满足的想法被视为异端。因为这个社会固执地认定我们只有置身于他人之中，才能完整。因为我们必须依附于他人来寻求慰藉、舒适和安全感。

可笑的是，我们大多数人所渴求的亲昵关系，已经超出了自己的承受能力。我们吝啬于给自己、伴侣和伙伴足够的空间，使其身心受到限制，然后，又对我们之间令人窒息的关系感到悲哀。

把这些事实指出来，并不是建议我们应该抛弃所有的亲密关系。医学调查证明，大多数老人独居，但与其亲朋好友保持着密切的联系，其身心健康的程度是"良好"。就像在他们年轻的时候，每天吃一个苹果可以不用看医生一样，一个积极的社交活动能产生同样的效果。

但是，我们需要在友好待人的同时，享受独处的乐趣。

我们必须重新学会独处，不要用永不停歇的音乐和漫不经心的聊天来充斥所有的空闲时间，而要培植孤独，让梦之花绽放。我们不能忍受寂静，仅仅只是想填满那个空白，因为，寂静包含了思考，如果我们思考，则必须面对自己。

让我们向探索者学习吧！然后发现他们尚未发现和拥有的东西：平和的心境，温和的性格，冷静的灵魂和平淡的快乐。要懂得如何去理解和热爱他人，对他人有价值，必须先了解自己，珍爱自己。要找到属于自己的道路，就必须从了解自我开始。

核心单词

solo ['səuləu] *adj.* 单独的

instinctively [in'stiŋktʃuəl] *adv.* (出于) 本能地；凭直觉

coin [kɔin] *n.* 硬币，钱币 *v.* 铸造 (货币)

ironically [ai'rɔnikli] *adv.* 说反话地；讽刺地

intimacy ['intiməsi] *n.* 熟悉；亲密；亲近

active ['æktiv] *adj.* 活跃的；活泼的

vacuum ['vækjuəm] *n.* 真空；空白，空虚

实用句型

Nonetheless, we persist in the conviction that a solitary existence is the harshest penalty life can mete out.

然而，我们坚持认为，独居是最残酷的生活方式。

①句中 that 引导的定语从句用来修饰 conviction。

② persist in 坚持不懈，执着，类似的表达还有 persist with 继续努力，坚持不懈等固定搭配。

翻译行不行

1. 水是由氢和氧组成的。(consists of)

....

2. 善恶自有报，只争迟与早。(mete out)

....

3. 香港被认为是以贸易和金融著称的城市。 (be viewed as)

....

Life Is Do-it-yourself Project

生活是一项为自己打造的工程

• Erma Bombeck •

An elderly carpenter was ready to **retire**. He told his employer of his plans to leave the house-building business and live a more **leisurely** life with his wife, enjoying his extended family. He would miss the paycheck, but he needed to retire. They could get by.

The employer was sorry to see his good worker go and asked if he could build just one more house as a personal favor. The carpenter said yes, but in time it was easy to see that his heart was not in his work. He resorted to shoddy workmanship and used **inferior** materials. It was an unfortunate way to end his career.

When the carpenter finished his work and the employer came to inspect the house and handed the front-door key to the carpenter. "This is your house," he said, "my gift to you."

What a shock! What a shame! If he had only known he was building his own house, he would have done it all so differently. Now he had to live in the home he had built none too well.

So it is with us. We build our lives in a distracted way,

reacting rather than acting, willing to put up less than the best. At important points we do not give the job our best effort. Then with a shock we look at the situation we have created and find that we are now living in the house we have built. *If we had realized, we would have done it differently.*

Think of yourself as the carpenter. Think about your house. Each day you hammer a nail, place a board, or erect a wall. Build wisely. It is the only life you will ever build. Even if you live it for only one day more, that day deserves to be lived graciously and with **dignity**. The **plaque** on the wall says, "Life is a do-it-yourself project." Who could say it more clearly? Your life tomorrow will be the result of your attitudes and the choices you make today.

埃尔马·邦贝克

一位上了年纪的木匠做好了退休的准备。他告诉老板他准备离开建筑行业，与老伴和儿孙们一起共享天伦之乐，过一种更悠然自得的生活。虽然他因此而少了份薪水，但他想退休了。至于日子嘛，还可以凑合着过。

眼看这位优秀的木工就要离去，老板很遗憾。他问木工可否帮忙再建一所房子。木工答应了，可明眼人一眼就看得出来，此时他做事心不在焉，做出的活儿技艺粗糙，用的料也没那么讲究了。他就这样为自己的建筑生涯画上了句号，真是令人遗憾。

房子建好后，老板过来看房并交给木工一把前门钥匙，说："这房子归你了，这是我送给你的礼物。"

多么令人吃惊，多么令人羞愧啊！假如他知道这房子是为自己造的，他会做得大不一样。现在他不得不住在自己建造的那所粗制滥造的房子里了。

我们又何尝不是如此呢？我们心浮气躁地打造生活，不是主动工作而是被动应付，能省事就省事，关键的时候也没尽心尽力。蓦然回首，才瞠目结舌地发现自己正住在自己建造的那所房子中，自食其果。早知如此，何必当初！

就当你自己是那位木工吧。就当你在为自己建房，每天要钉钉、铺板、砌墙。如果你能这么想，那么你就用心地去建，而且你的生活也只能这样建造。哪怕你在房子里只生活一天，这一天也应该活得优雅而有尊严。墙上的铭匾写道："生活是一项为自己打造的工程。"还有什么比这更清楚的呢？明日的生活之果，孕育自你今天的态度和抉择之树上。

核心单词

retire [ri'taiəd] *v.* 退休；退役

leisurely ['leʒəli] *adj.* 从容不迫的，悠闲的

inferior [in'fiəriə] *adj.* 低等的；下级的；低于

dignity ['digniti] *n.* 尊严；庄严

plaque [plɑ:k] *n.* 铭牌；徽章

实用句型

If we had realized, we would have done it differently.

早知如此，何必当初。

①这里是虚拟语气的 if + had done 形式，表示与现在事实相反的假设。

② differently 不同地，类似的由形容词 +ly 构成的副词还有 pleasantly 愉快地；slowly 缓慢地；carefully 仔细地；suddenly 意外地等。

翻译行不行

1. 下岗后，他经常借酒消愁。(resort to)

....

2. 他们及时赶上了公共汽车。(in time)

....

3. 请看这张地图。(look at)

....

灰色晨曦中，那通往 彩虹 的路

In grey dawn, the road to somewhere over the rainbow

J.K.Rowling, Author of Harry Potter
哈利波特的缔造者——J·K·罗琳

Like that of her own character, Harry Potter, J.K. Rowling's life has the **luster** of a fairy tale. Divorced, living on public assistance in a tiny Edinburgh flat with her infant daughter, Rowling wrote *Harry Potter and the Sorcerers' Stone* at a table in a cafe during her daughter's naps — and it was Harry Potter that **rescued** her.

Joanne Kathleen Rowling entered the world in Chipping Sodbury General Hospital in Bristol, England, a fitting beginning for someone who would later enjoy making up strange names for people, places and games played on flying broomsticks. Her younger sister Di was born just under two years later.

Rowling remembers that she always wanted to write and that the first story she actually wrote down, when she was five or six, was a story about a rabbit called Rabbit. Many of her favorite memories center around reading—hearing *The Wind in the Willows* read aloud by her father when she had the measles, enjoying the **fantastic** adventure stories of E. Nesbit, reveling in the magical world of C. S. Lewis's Narnia, and her favorite story of all, *The Little White Horse* by Elizabeth Goudge.

At Exeter University Rowling took her degree in French and spent one year studying in Paris. After college she moved to London to work for Amnesty International as a researcher and bilingual secretary. The best thing about working in an office, she has said, was typing up stories on the computer when no one was watching. During this time, on a particularly long train ride from Manchester to London in the summer of 1990, the idea came to her of a boy who is a **wizard** and doesn't know it. He attends a school for wizardry—she could see him very **plainly** in her mind. By the time the train pulled into King's Cross Station four hours later, many of the characters and the early stages of the plot were fully formed in her head. The story took further shape as she continued working on it in pubs and cafes over her lunch hours.

In 1992 Rowling left off working in offices and moved to Portugal to teach English as a Second Language. *In spite of her students making jokes about her name (this time they called her "Rolling Stone"), she enjoyed teaching.* She worked afternoons and evenings, leaving mornings free for writing. After her marriage to a Portuguese TV journalist ended in divorce, Rowling returned to Britain with her infant daughter and a suitcase full of Harry Potter notes and chapters. She settled in Edinburgh to be near her sister and set out to finish the book before looking for a teaching job. Wheeling her daughter's carriage around the city to escape their tiny, cold apartment, she would duck into coffee shops to write when the baby fell asleep. In this way she finished the book and started sending it to publishers. It was **rejected** several times before she found London agent, chosen because

In grey dawn, the road to somewhere over the rainbow

灰色晨曦中，那通往彩虹的路

she liked his name—Christopher Little, who sold the manuscript to Bloomsbury Children's Books.

Rowling was working as a French teacher when she heard that her book about the boy wizard had been accepted for publication. *Harry Potter and the Philosopher's Stone* was published in June 1997 and achieved almost instant success. With the publication of the American edition, retitled *Harry Potter and the Sorcerer's Stone*, in 1998, Rowling's books continued to make publishing history. *Harry Potter* climbed to the top of all the bestseller lists for children's and adult books. Indeed, the story of the boy wizard, his Cinderlad childhood, and his **adventures** at Hogwarts School of Witchcraft and Wizardry caught the imagination of readers of all ages. In Britain a separate edition of the first book appeared with a more "adult" dust **jacket** so that grown-ups reading it on trains and subways would not have to hide their copy behind a newspaper.

J.K. Rowling lives in Edinburgh, Scotland, with her daughter Jessica and continues to work on writing the seven-book saga of *Harry Potter*.

史蒂文

J·K·罗琳的生活展现出童话般的光芒，如同她所创造的魔法小巫师——哈利·波特。经历了一次失败的婚姻后，这个靠救济金过日子，独自抚养女儿的单亲妈妈和出生不久的女儿搬到了爱丁堡的一个狭小的公寓里。她常待在住家附近的咖啡馆里，待女儿熟睡后开始写作，女儿睡多久，她就写多久。就在这个小咖啡馆里，她写出了《哈利波特与魔法石》，塑造了那个将她带离窘境的小巫师。

出生在英格兰的一家综合医院里，这对一个喜欢给别人起奇怪的名字，喜欢坐着扫帚满场飞奔的小姑娘来说，是个合适的开始。她的妹妹娣，比她小两岁。

罗琳从小就喜欢写作，五六岁时就写了一篇跟兔子有关的故事。小时候美好的记忆似乎总是围绕阅读的——得麻疹时听爸爸大声讲《柳林风声》，读 E·尼斯比特奇异的冒险故事，沉浸在 C.S. 路易斯的奇妙的纳尼亚传奇的故事世界里。不过，她最喜欢还是伊丽莎白·古吉的《古堡里的月亮公主》。

在 Exeter 大学里，罗琳主修法语并在巴黎留学一年。毕业后，她搬去伦敦担任国际特赦组织的调查员和双语秘书。罗琳回忆说，那段时间最有趣的事情就是趁没人的时候在电脑上打小说。1990 年的夏天，当罗琳坐在由曼彻斯特出发前往伦敦的火车上时，哈利波特闯入了她的世界。她可以在脑海里清晰地勾画他的模样，看到他进入魔法学校。四小时后，当火车驶入王十字车站时，大部分人物和故事的前期框架已经在她的脑海里形成了。当她午餐时间坐在咖啡馆里继续构思时，故事的结构变得更加清晰了。

1992 年，罗琳结束了白领生涯，前往葡萄牙做英语教师。尽管学生们常拿她的名字开玩笑，叫她滚石（英语中 Rowling 与 Rolling 同音），她仍然非常喜欢教书。她在下午和晚上去学校工作，上午用来写作。不久后，她与一名葡萄牙的电视台记者结婚，但这段婚姻最终以离婚告终。离婚后，罗琳带着女儿和满满一箱子哈利波特的笔记与手稿回到了英国。为了能离妹妹近一些，罗琳在爱丁堡定居下来，准备在找新工作前完成这部小说。她常常推着女儿的手推车四处闲逛，只是为了逃离那又小又冷的公寓。她会躲到咖啡馆里，趁女儿睡着时写作。就这样，罗琳完成了哈利波特的创作并开始寻找出版商。但她的稿件多次被退了回来，直到她找到了一个伦敦的经纪人。罗琳之所以会找到他，仅仅是因为喜欢他可爱的名字——克里斯多夫·里特，他将原稿卖给了布鲁斯伯里出版社。

当罗琳得知这本关于小巫师的小说被出版商接受时，她正在一所学校教法语。《哈利波特和巫师的石头》在 1997 年 6 月刚一出版，就大获成功。随着更名为《哈利波特和神秘的魔法石》，1998 年在美国的出版，罗琳的书继续创造着出版界的历史。《哈利波特》登上了儿童与成人书籍的最佳销售榜的首位。确实，这个小巫师的故事，他灰姑娘一样的童年，和他在霍格华兹魔法学校的历险引发了各个年龄段读者的丰富想象力。在英国，出版商出版了一种更成人化封面的版本，使得大人们能在火车或者地铁里阅读而不用把书藏在报纸后面。

现在，J·K·罗琳和她的女儿捷西卡住在苏格兰的爱丁堡，继续完成 7 本《哈利波特》的冒险故事。

Practising
& Exercise

実战
提升篇

核心单词

luster ['lʌstə] *n.* 光泽；光辉；光彩

rescue ['reskju:] *v.* 援救；营救；挽救

fantastic [fæn'tæstik] *adj.* 想像中的，奇异的；古怪的

wizard ['wizəd] *n.* 男巫；术士

plainly ['pleinli] *adv.* 清楚地，明显地；明确地

reject [ri'dʒekt] *v.* 拒绝，抵制

adventure [əd'ventʃə] *n.* 冒险，冒险精神

jacket ['dʒækit] *n.* 夹克，上衣

实用句型

In spite of her students making jokes about her name, she enjoyed teaching.

尽管学生们常拿她的名字开玩笑，叫她滚石（英语中 Rowling 与 rolling 同音），她仍然非常喜欢教书。

① In spite of 在这里引导让步状语从句。

② making jokes about her name 以她的名字为笑柄，类似的表达还有 make a joke 开玩笑；be but a joke 只是笑话；no joke 不是闹着玩的等固定搭配。

翻译行不行

1. 请尽快戒掉你的坏习惯。(leave off)

....

2. 那项计划以失败而告终。(end in)

....

3. 我还没有适应我的新工作。(settle in)

....

The God in Youth: Michael Jordan
少年天才——迈克尔·乔丹

• Leander •

There were already signs that he had a good deal of talent. Harvest Smith, a classmate and close friend who in those days played basketball with him **practically** every day, thought he was the best player on their ninth-grade team — he was small, but he was very quick. "You'd see him get a shot off, and you'd wonder how he did it, because he wasn't that big," Smith said, "but it was the quickness. The only question was how big he was going to be — and how far up he would take his skill level."

The summer after ninth grade, Jordan and Smith both went to Pop Herring's basketball camp. Neither of them had yet come into his body, and almost all of the varsity players, two and sometimes three years older, seemed **infinitely** stronger at that moment when a year or two in physical development can make all the difference. In Smith's mind there was no doubt which of the two of them was the better player—it was Michael by far. But on the day the varsity cuts were announced — it was the big day of the year, for they had all known for weeks when the list would be posted — he and Roy Smith had gone to the Laney gym. Smith's name was on it, Michael's was not.

It was the worst day of Jordan's young life. The list was alphabetical, so he focused on where the Js should be, and it wasn't there, and he kept reading and rereading the list, hoping somehow that he had missed it, or that the alphabetical listing had been done incorrectly. That day he went home by himself and went to his room and cried. Smith understood what was happening—Michael, he knew, never wanted you to see him when he was hurt.

"We knew Michael was good," Fred Lynch, the Laney **assistant** coach, said later, "but we wanted him to play more and we thought the JV was better for him." He easily became the best player on the JV that year. He simply **dominated** the play, and he did it not by size but with quickness. There were games in which he would score forty points. He was so good, in fact, that the JV games became quite popular. *The entire varsity began to come early so they could watch him play in the JV games.*

Smith noticed that while Jordan had been wildly **competitive** before he had been cut, after the cut he seemed even more competitive than ever, as if determined that it would never happen again. His coaches noticed it, too. "The first time I ever saw him, I had no idea who Michael Jordan was. I was helping to coach the Laney varsity," said Ron Coley. "We went over to Goldsboro, which was our big **rival,** and I entered the gym when the jayvee game was just ending up. There were nine players on the court just coasting, but there was one kid playing his heart out. The way he was playing I thought his team was down one

In grey dawn, the road to somewhere over the rainbow

灰色晨曦中，那通往彩虹的路

point with two minutes to play. So I looked up at the clock and his team was down twenty points and there was only one minute to play. It was Michael, and I quickly learned he was always like that."

Between the time he was cut and the start of basketball in his junior year, Jordan grew about four inches. The speed had always been there, and now he was stronger, and he could dunk. His hands had gotten much bigger, Smith noticed. He was as driven as ever, the hardest-working player on the team in practice. If he thought that his teammates were not working hard enough, he would get on them himself, and on occasion he pushed the coaches to get on them. Suddenly Laney High had the beginning of a very good basketball team, and its rising star was Michael Jordan.

利安德尔

迈克尔的天赋早已有所显露。他的一位同班同学和亲密伙伴维斯特·史密斯，当时基本每天都和他一起打篮球，他认为乔丹是九年级球队中最出色的——他身材不高但非常灵活。史密斯说："你看到他盖帽儿，就想问问他是怎么盖的，因为他没那么高大，可他身手敏捷。唯一的问题是他将会长多高，他的技能会提高到什么程度。"

读完九年级的那个夏天，乔丹和史密斯一同参加了波谱·赫里的篮球夏令营。他们俩在当时还未长大成人，而当时几乎所有的校队队员都比他们大两三岁，在这个年龄段，大一两岁在体魄上就大相径庭，因而看上去都比他们强壮得多。在史密斯的头脑中，他们两人谁更出色是毫无疑问的——迈克尔比他要强得多。但是到了宣布校运动队队员筛选名单时——这可是一年中的大日子，因为他们几星期前就知道名单何时会公布——他和罗伊·史密斯都去了兰尼体育馆，发现名单上有史密斯的名字，却没有迈克尔。

对于年轻的乔丹来说这一天简直糟透了。因为名单是按字母顺序排列的，他就注意看可能有"乔"字的地方，可是没有。他一遍又一遍地找，真希望是自己看漏了，或者是字母顺序排错了。那天他独自回了家进屋后便大哭起来。史密斯明白所发生的一切——当迈克尔伤心或沮丧的时候，他不愿意见人。

兰尼的助理教练里德·里奇后来说："我们知道迈克尔很出色，但我们想让他多练练，所以觉得二队更适合他。"那一年他轻松地成了二队中最出色的队员。凭借着敏捷而非身高，他在队中就已举足轻重。许多比赛他都能得到 40 分。实际上他突出的表现使二队的比赛倍受欢迎。为了能看到有他参加的二队比赛，整个校队的队员都开始提早到场。

史密斯发现在乔丹被筛选掉之前是不甘于人后的，而在落选之后他的好胜心似乎有过之而无不及，好像决心不让历史再次重演。他的教练们也注意到了这一点。罗·康利说："我一直在兰尼的运动队做教练，当我第一次看到迈克尔·乔丹时，还不知道他是谁。我们去与劲敌哥尔兹保罗队打比赛，当我进到体育馆时，二队的比赛就要结束了。场上的九名队员都已无心恋战，只剩下一个孩子还在竭尽全力。看他打球的样子我想他们队在剩下的两分钟里一定只落后了一分，可当我抬头看计时钟时，他们队在最后的一分钟里竟落后了二十分。这就是迈克尔，我很快就得知他一贯如此。"

从乔丹少年时开始打篮球到被筛选掉的这段时间，他长了四英寸。他的速度仍然是那么快，只是现在他健壮了许多并且也能扣篮了。史密斯注意到，他的手也大了不少。他一直都充满着紧迫感，他是队中最勤于练球的队员。倘若他发现队友不够努力，他就会亲自去说服他们，或者鼓动教练去。一时间兰尼中学出了一个非常优秀的篮球队，迈克尔·乔丹成了冉冉升起的明星。

Practising & Exercise 实战提升篇

核心单词

practically ['præktikəli] v. 几乎，差不多

infinitely ['infinitli] adv. 无限地，无穷地；极其

assistant [ə'sistənt] n. 助手，店员；adj. 助理的；辅助的

dominate ['dɔmineit] v. 支配，统治，控制

competitive [kəm'petitiv] adj. 竞争的；竞争性的

rival ['raivəl] n. 竞争者，对手，敌手

实用句型

The entire varsity began to come early so they could watch him play in the JV games.

为了能看到有他参加的二队比赛，整个校队的队员都开始提前到场。

①这是由 so 引导的结果状语从句。

② begin to 开始，着手，动手，类似的表达还有 begin with 以……开始等固定搭配。

翻译行不行

1. 我确信我最终会成功。（no doubt）

....

2. 她是公司中最为优秀的决策人之一。（by far）

....

3. 大庭广众之下要注意言行。（on occasion）

....

Three Days to See
假如给我三天光明

• Helen Keller •

All of us have read thrilling stories in which the hero had only a limited and specified time to live. Sometimes it was as long as a year, sometimes as short as twenty-four hours, but always we were interested in discovering just how the doomed man chose to spend his last years or his last hours. I speak, of course, of free men who have a choice, not condemned criminals whose sphere of activities is strictly limited.

Such stories set up thinking, wondering what we should do under similar circumstances. What associations should we crowd into those last hours as mortal beings? What happiness should we find in reviewing the past, what regrets?

Sometimes I have thought it would be an excellent rule to live each day as if we should die tomorrow. Such an attitude would emphasize sharply the values of life. We should live each day with a gentleness, a vigor, and a keenness of appreciation on which are often lost when times stretches before us in the constant panorama of more days and months and years to come. There are those, of course, who would adopt the epicurean motto of "eat, drink, and be merry," most people would be

chastened by the certainty of impending death.

Most of us take life for granted. We know that one day we must die, but usually we picture that day as far in the future, when we are in buoyant health, death is all but unimaginable. We seldom think of it. The days stretch out in an endless vista. So we go about our petty tasks, hardly aware of our listless attitude towards life.

The same lethargy,I am afraid,characterizes the use of our faculties and senses. Only the deaf appreciate hearing, only the blind realize the manifold blessings that lie in sight. Particularly does this observation apply to those who have lost sight and hearing in adult life. But those who have never suffered **impairment** of sight or hearing seldom make the fullest use of these blessed faculties. Their eyes and ears take in all sights and sound hazily, without concentration, and with little appreciation. It is the same old story of not being grateful for our health until we are ill...

Now and then I have tested my seeing friends to discover what they see. Recently I was visited by a very good friend who had just returned from a long walk in the woods, and I asked her what she had **observed**. "Nothing in particular," She replied. I might have been **incredulous** had I not been accustomed to such responses, for long ago I became convinced that the seeing see little.

How was it possible, I asked myself, to walk for an hour through the woods and see nothing worthy of note? I who cannot see find hundreds of things to interest me through mere touch. I feel the delicate **symmetry** of a leaf. I pass my hands lovingly about the smooth skin of a silver birch, or the rough shaggy bark of a pine. In spring I touch the branches of trees hopefully in search of a bud, the first sign of awakening Nature after her winter's sleep.

I feel the delightful, velvety texture of a flower, and discover its remarkable convolutions; and something of the miracle of Nature is revealed to me. Occasionally, if I am very fortunate, I place my hand gently in a small tree and feel the happy quiver of a bird in full song. I am delighted to have cool waters of a brook rush through my open fingers. To me a lush carpet of pine needles or spongy grass is more welcome than the most luxurious Persian rug. To me the pageant of seasons is a thrilling and unending drama, the action of which streams through my finger tips. At times my heart cries out with longing to see all these things. If I can get so much pleasure from mere touch, how much more beauty must be revealed by sight. Yet, those who have eyes **apparently** see little. The panorama of color and action filling the world is taken for granted. It is Human, perhaps, to appreciate little that which we have and to long for that which we have not, but it is a great pity that in the world of light the gift of sight is used only as mere convenience rather than as a means of adding fullness to life.

Oh, the things that I should see if I had the power of sight for three days!

海伦·凯勒

所有人都读过动人的故事，故事中的英雄将不久于人世，长则一年，短则 24 小时。但我们经常关注的是这个命中注定要死的人如何选择度过生命中的最后几天或是最后几个小时。当然，我在这里所说的是有权做出选择的自由人，而并非那些活动范围受到严格限制的死囚。

这类故事会激发起我们的思考：倘若身处类似的环境下，我们自己该做些什么？在那临终前的几个小时里我们会产生哪些联想？会有多少欣慰和遗憾呢？

有时我想，把每天都当作生命的最后一天来度过也不失为一种好的生命法则。这种态度重视的是人生的价值。每一天我们都应该以和善的态度、充沛的精力和热情的欣赏来度过，但当时间展现在我们面前、来日方长的时候，我们会忽视这些东西。当然，有一些人奉行享乐主义的座右铭——吃喝玩乐，但大多数人却依然畏惧死亡的到来。

我们大多数人都认为生命是理所当然的，明白自己终有一天会死去，但却常常把这一天看得非常遥远。当我们身体强健的时候，死亡变成了难以想象的事情。我们很少考虑死亡，日子也一天天过去，好像永无尽头，所以我们为琐事奔波，而并没有意识到我们对待生活的态度是冷漠的。

我想我们在运用所有的五官时恐怕也同样是冷漠的。只有聋子才珍惜听力，只有盲人才能认识到能见光明的幸运。对于那些成年失明或失聪的人尤其如此。但那些听力或视力未见损失的人却很少充分利用这些幸运的能力，他们对所见所闻不关注，不欣赏。这与常说的不失去不知珍惜、不生病不知健康可贵的道理是一样的。

我时常考问我的有视力的朋友，以了解他们看到了什么。最近有一个很好的朋友在长时间林中漫步之后来看我，我问她观察到了些什么。"没什么特别的。"她回答道。要不是我已习惯于类似的反应，我也许会感到难以置信。我之所以不觉得奇怪是因为我早就确信：有视力者所见甚少。

我想，这怎么可能！在林中走了一个小时，却什么值得注意的东西都没有看到吗？而我一个盲人仅仅通过触觉便发现了数以百计的有趣的东西。我感到树叶的对称美，用手抚摸着白桦树光滑的树皮或是松树那厚厚的粗糙的外衣。春天里我满怀希望地触摸着树枝寻找新芽，那是大自然的冬眠后醒来的第一个征象。我感到了花朵的可爱以及它那天鹅绒般柔软的质地，发现它层层叠叠地绽放着，大自然的神奇就在我的面前。我把手轻轻地放在一棵小树上，如果幸运的话，偶尔会感到歌唱着的小鸟正欢快地颤动。我会让清凉的溪水从手指间流过，而对我来说，满地厚厚的松针和松软的草坪比奢华的波斯地毯更惹人喜爱，四季变幻的景色也仿佛是一场动人心魄永不会完结的戏剧，剧中的人物动作从我的指尖流过。我的心在不时地呐喊，带着对光明的渴望。如果仅是通过触摸就可以使我获得如此多的喜悦，那么光明定会向我展示更多美好的事物啊。可惜那些眼未失明的人分明看到很少，整个世界缤纷的色彩和万物的活动都被认为是理所当然的。也许不珍惜已经拥有的，想得到还没有得到的是人类的本性，但是在光明的世界里，视觉只是作为一种方便的工具，而不是丰富生活的工具存在，这是多么令人遗憾的事情啊！

噢，假如我拥有三天的光明，我将会看到多少美好的事物啊！

核心单词

chasten ['tʃeisn] v. 磨炼；抑制，节制

impairment [im'pɛəmənt] n. 损伤

observe [əb'zə:v] v. 看到，注意到

incredulous [in'kredjuləs] adj. 不轻信的；怀疑的

symmetry ['simitri] n. 对称（性）；匀称；整齐

apparently [ə'pærəntli] adv. 显然地；表面上，似乎

实用句型

The same lethargy，I am afraid,characterizes the use of our faculties and senses.

我想我们在运用所有的五官时恐怕也同样是冷漠的。

①I am afraid 在这里是插入语。

②I am afraid 恐怕，类似的插入语还有 you see；that is to say 等。

翻译行不行

1. 别把迟到视为理所当然。(take for granted)

....

2. 朋友们偶尔聚会，畅谈学生时代的美好时光。(now and then)

....

3. 我一直在寻找一个能理解我的人。(in search of)

....

Bill Gates in His Boyhood
少年比尔·盖茨

· Leopold ·

As a child—and an adult as well—Bill was untidy. It has been said that in order to counteract this. Mary drew up weekly clothing plans for him. On Mondays he might go to school in blue, on Tuesdays in green, on Wednesdays in brown , on Thursdays in black, and so on , Weekend meal **schedules** might also be planned in detail. Everything time, at work or during his leisure time, Bill hated wasting time.

Dinner table discussions in the Gate's family home were always lively and educational. "It was a rich environment in which to learn," Bill remembered.

Bill's contemporaries, even at that age, recognized that he was exceptional. Every year, he and his friends would go to summer camp. Bill **especially** liked swimming and other sports. One of his summer camp friends recalled, "He was never a nerd or a goof or the kind of kid you didn't want on your team. We all knew Bill was smarter than us. Even back then, when he was nine or ten years old, he talked like an adult and could express himself in ways that none of us understood."

Bill was also well ahead of his classmates in mathematics and science. He needed to go to a school that challenged him to Lakeside—an all boys' school for exceptional students. It was Seattle's most exclusive school and was noted for its **rigorous** academic demands, a place where "even the dumb kids were smart."

Lakeside allowed students to pursue their own interests, to whatever extent they wished. The school prided itself on making conditions and facilities available that would enable all its students to reach their full potential. It was the ideal environment for someone like Bill Gates.

In 1968, the school made a decision that would change thirteen-year-old Bill Gates's life—and that of many of others, too.

Funds were raised, mainly by parents, that enabled the school to gain access to a computer—a Program Data processor(PDP)—through a teletype machine. Type in a few instructions on the teletype machine and a few seconds later the PDP would type back its response. Bill Gates was immediately hooked—so was his best friend at the time, Kent Evans, and another student, Paul Allen, who was two years older than Bill.

Whenever they had free time, and sometimes when they didn't, they would **dash** over to the computer room to use the machine. The students became so single-minded that they soon **overtook** their teachers in knowledge about computing and got into a lot of trouble because of their obsession. They were **neglecting** their other studies—every piece of work was handed in late. Classes

灰色晨曦中，那通往彩虹的路

were cut. Computer time was also proving to be very expensive. Within months, the whole budget that had been set aside for the year had been used up.

At fourteen, Bill was already writing short programs for the computer to perform. Early games programs such as Tic-Tac-Toe, or Noughts and Crosses, and Lunar Landing were written in what was to become Bill's second language, BASIC.

One of the reasons Bill was so good at programming is because it is mathematical and logical. During his time at Lakeside, Bill **scored** a perfect eight hundred on a mathematics test. It was extremely important to him to get this grade—he had to take the test more than once in order to do it.

If Bill Gates was going to be good at something. It was essential to be the best.

Bill's and Paul's fascination with computers and the business world meant that they read a great deal. Paul enjoyed magazines like *Popular Electronics* while Bill liked the business ones. Computer time was expensive and, because both boys were desperate to get more time and because Bill already had an **insight** into what they could achieve financially, the two of them decided to set themselves up as a company: The Lakeside Programmers Group. "Let's call the real world and try to sell something to it!" Bill **announced**.

利奥波特

童年时期——即使成了大人——比尔也不修边幅。据说为了改此习惯，玛丽为他制定了一周的着装计划。周一上学时穿蓝色装，周二绿色，周三棕色，周四黑色，等等。周末的用餐时间也安排得井井有条。比尔·盖茨讨厌浪费时间，无论是在工作中或闲暇时。

在比尔家的餐桌上的讨论总是既生动又富有教育意义。"那是个内容丰富的学习环境，"比尔回忆道。

比尔的同龄人，即使是在那个年龄，都能看出他的与众不同。每年，他和朋友们都要去夏令营。比尔特别喜爱游泳或其他的运动。他在夏令营的一位朋友回忆道，"他绝不会是个不足挂齿或无足轻重之人。我们都晓得比尔比我们聪颖。甚至在更早的时候，当他10来岁时，言谈就如同成人一般，他说的话有时我们感到高深莫测。

在数学和自然科学方面比尔比同班同学也更胜一筹。他需要上一所对他充满挑战的学校。随即父母决定送他去湖畔中学——一所专门招收超常男生的学校。这是西雅图一所限制最严的学校，它以严格的课程要求而著称，是个"连哑童都聪明的"地方。

湖畔中学允许学生们按自己兴趣自由发挥，去通达他们希望的极致。令校方骄傲的是他们所创造的环境及设施使学生们能充分发挥各自的潜能。这是像比尔·盖茨这样学生的理想环境。

1968年，学校做出的一项决定改变了13岁的比尔·盖茨的生活——同时也改变了许多其他的人。

学校主要靠家长提供的资金通过一种电传打字机进入电脑——即程序数据处理机。在电传打字机上键入几条指令，几秒钟后程序数据处理机即会反馈回信息。比尔·盖茨当即就着了迷——他那时最要好的朋友坎特·埃文斯和另一名长他两岁的同学保罗·艾伦也是如此。

他们不管有没有空，都要赶到电脑室去用用那台机器。这些学生非常地专注，以至于在电脑方面的知识都超过了老师，同时因为他们的执著也带来了不少麻烦。他们忽略了其他的课程——每项作业都未按时交，有时还旷课。上机的费用也很昂贵。几个月后，当初留做一年用的预算就已经消耗殆尽了。

比尔 14 岁时，就已开始编写简短的电脑运行程序了。早期的游戏程序如"三棋杀三子"，或"画圈打叉游戏"，及"登月"就是用后来成为比尔的第二种语言 BASIC 来写的。

比尔善于编程的其中一个原因就是它蕴含的运算性与逻辑性。他在湖畔中学的那段时间，比尔在一次数学测验中取得了满分 800 分，取得这样的成绩对他来说是至关重要的——为了这个成绩他不得不参加几次测验。

倘若比尔·盖茨决定要做好某件事，他必定会做得最为出色。

比尔和保罗对电脑和商务的痴迷意味着他们要博览群书。保罗喜爱像《大众电子》之类的刊物，而比尔则翻阅商业杂志。上机时间的昂贵，以及因为这两个孩子迫切需要更多的上机时间，还有比尔早已洞察到他们在经济上会有所收益，于是他们俩决定组建自己的公司：湖畔程序设计者集团。比尔宣布道："让我们唤醒这个世界并给它推销点东西吧！"

核心单词

schedule ['ʃedjuːl] *n.* 清单；目录；时间表；课程表

especially [is'peʃəli] *adv.* 特别；尤其；格外

rigorous ['rigərəs] *adj.* 严格的；严厉的；苛刻的

dash [dæʃ] *v.* 猛撞；猛砸；击碎

overtake [əuvə'teik] *v.* 追上；赶上；超过

neglect [ni'glekt] *v.* 忽视，忽略；疏忽

score [skɔː] *n.* (比赛中的)得分，比数；(测验的)成绩

insight ['insait] *n.* 洞察力，眼光

announce [ə'nauns] *v.* 宣布，发布

实用句型

As a child—and an adult as well—Bill was untidy.

童年时期——即使成了大人——比尔也一样不修边幅。

① As a child—and an adult 介词短语与 bill 并行，并对其进行修饰。

② and...as well 也，又，同样地；类似的表达还有 as well as 不但……而且；might as well 该……做；just as well 幸好，无妨等固定搭配。

翻译行不行

1. 您能否详细地说明一下主题？(in detail)

....

2. 他每月都留出一些钱备用。(set aside)

....

3. 她擅长人物素描。(be good at)

....

Oprah Winfrey, a Refulgent Soul
逆风飞扬

• Terry •

Oprah Winfrey is one of the most exciting, highest paid, and best-loved celebrities in America. She is also the country's top television talk show host. Oprah Winfrey is a very fine actress and a successful producer. She is a living example of what talent, hard work, and determination can do.

Oprah Winfrey has come a long way from her poor childhood home in a small Mississippi town. She was an unwanted child whose parents never married. She was brought up on her grandmother's farm. The **possibility** that she would become rich and famous was not very good.

Oprah's mother left her child in her mother's care, so she could go to work in Milwaukee, Wisconsin. It was a strict and difficult life for Oprah. But it also led the way for her future. She was a highly **intelligent** child. By the age of three, she had learned to read and write. She also made her first public appearance at that age. She gave a talk in church, which impressed everyone. "That child is gifted," people said.

Oprah's intelligence was resented by other children her age.

They called her unkind names and pushed her away. Oprah felt very **isolated** and unwanted. It made her feel worse that she didn't live with her mother and father. She felt that no one loved her. This made her angry, resentful, and rebellious. These feelings brought her much trouble as she was growing up. She often **behaved** badly, causing her grandmother to punish her. By the time Oprah was seven, she was too much for her grandmother to discipline. Then Oprah went to live with her mother, Vernita, in Milwaukee.

Vernita worked very hard at her job as a housekeeper. It was hard for her to work and take care of her bright, troublesome child. Oprah was a burden, and she knew it. They lived in poverty in a small apartment in the city. Oprah took out all her angry feelings on her mother. She was a difficult child. When Oprah was eight, Vernita sent her to live with her father and **stepmother** in Nashville, Tennessee. But she moved again a few months later when Vernita married a man with two children. Vernita wanted Oprah with her and her new family.

Unfortunately she felt she didn't belong with them. She believed she wasn't loved by anyone. Her anger and **frustration** grew stronger. She struck back by misbehaving and running away from home. Her parents found her impossible to discipline. When she was 14 they tried to send her to a special center for troubled girls. But there was no room for her. So Vernita sent Oprah back to live with her father. Vernon Winfrey was by then a successful businessman and family man. He took one look at his daughter and knew she needed guidance, love, and discipline.

He gave her all three. It was a turning point in Oprah's life. Vernon Winfrey was strict about his daughter's education. He gave her homework in addition to her schoolwork. She was allowed to watch only one hour of television a day. She became an A student and a popular girl in her class.

Oprah watched Barbara Walters, a famous journalist and interviewer, and decided that was what she wanted to be. When she was still in high school, she got a part-time job reading news on the radio. In her senior year she won a beauty contest and a four-year scholarship to Tennessee State University. While still in college she was offered a job as a news broadcaster at a local television station. She was the first female and the first African-American newscaster in Nashville. She was promoted to anchor, the most important position on the news team, while still a senior.

After Oprah graduated she got a job with a Baltimore news station. But she soon realized that broadcasting news wasn't enough for her. She had to let her personality shine through. She wanted to show emotion when she told a story, not just report it. Meanwhile the station managers were thinking the same way. They couldn't stop her from commenting on the news she read. They **removed** her from the anchor spot and wondered what to do with her. Finally they put her on an early morning talk show called *People Are Talking*. No one knew what to expect.

The show was a great success. In a very short time, the managers and Oprah all knew what she was born to do. She was funny, **witty**, charming, warm, and compassionate. She was everything a talk show host should be. *She was so successful that she got a show with a bigger station in Chicago.* It was called A. M. Chicago. Within one month the show's ratings were the best in years. Twice she left the show to make movies, *The Color Purple and Native Son*. In 1985 the show was changed to *The Oprah Winfrey Show*. It was broadcast nationally and soon became the most popular talk show on television . By the age of 35, Oprah Winfrey was one of the most famous celebrities in America.

特 里

奥普拉·温弗瑞是美国最令人激动的、薪水最高的和最受喜爱的知名人士之一，她还是美国顶级脱口秀节目主持人、非常优秀的女演员和成功的制片人。（要问）才华、勤奋和决心能成就什么，她就是一个鲜活的例子。

奥普拉·温弗瑞来自遥远的密西西比一个小镇贫穷的家庭。她是父母的非婚生子，在外婆的农场里长大成人，发财和成名的可能性都非常之小。

奥普拉·温弗瑞的妈妈把自己的孩子交给妈妈看管，这样，她就能去威斯康星的米尔瓦基工作。生活对奥普拉·温弗瑞来说既严格又艰难，但这引领她走向了属于她的未来。她是个非常聪明的孩子。三岁时，已经学会了读书认字，并第一次在舞台上公开演出。奥普拉·温弗瑞在教堂的讲话，给人们留下了很好的印象，人们都说她"这孩子很有天赋"。

奥普拉·温弗瑞的聪明遭到了同龄孩子的嫉恨。他们辱骂她，排斥她。奥普拉·温弗瑞感到孤独无助。不能和爸爸妈妈住在一起使她心情更糟，她感到没人喜欢她。这一切造就了她愤怒、怨恨和反叛的性格。随着年龄的增长，这给她带来了很多麻烦。她经常不守规矩，招来外婆的惩罚。七岁时，外婆再也管不了她了。后来，奥普拉就去和在米尔瓦基的妈妈——沃尼塔一起生活。

给人做女管家，沃尼塔干得非常卖力。既要工作又要照顾她那聪明而又常惹事生非的孩子使她很作难，奥普拉也感觉到自己是妈妈的负担。她们住在市里的一个小公寓里，日子过得很清贫。奥普拉将所有的火气都发到了妈妈的身上，孩子成了沃尼塔的一大麻烦。奥普拉八岁时，妈妈把她送到了田纳西州的那斯维尔（Nashville）的生父和继母那里。后来，沃尼塔又和一个带有两个孩子的男人结了婚，又把奥普拉接了回来，因为沃尼塔想要奥普拉与她和她的新家在一起。

不幸的是，奥普拉感到自己不属于这个家，她觉得谁也不爱她。她的愤恨与挫折感越发强烈，就用不守规矩和离家出走来进行反击。她的爸爸妈妈觉得无望管教好他们的女儿，14岁那年试图把她送到麻烦女孩的特别中心。但那里已经没有地方了，于是沃尼塔又把她送到她爸爸那里去。佛蒙·温弗瑞当时已经再婚，并且是一位成功的商人。他观察了他的女儿，了解到她需要引导、爱和管教。她需要的，他都给予了，这成了奥普拉人生的转折点。佛蒙·温弗瑞对女儿的教育要求非常严格，除学校的作业外，他还给她布置家庭作业，一天只允许她看一个小时的电视。奥普拉成了班上最优秀的学生，成了班里受欢迎的女孩。

奥普拉看到了著名的新闻记者和采访人芭芭拉·瓦尔特丝，决心成为像她那样的人。上高中时，就兼职在广播电台播新闻。高年级时，她在一次选美大赛中胜出，赢取了田纳西州立大学四年的助学金。到了大学时期，她在当地一家电视台播报新闻。她是那斯维尔市获取这种工作的第一位女性和第一位美国黑人。大学四年级时，奥普拉晋升为新闻播报负责人，这是新闻组最重要的位置。

大学毕业后，奥普拉在巴尔的摩电视台谋得工作。她很快不满足于播报新闻，想要充分展示自己的个性，满怀激情的讲述而非简单地播送。与此同时，电视台的经理也在琢磨这个问题。他们无法阻拦她播送新闻时的评论。他们将她调离新闻负责人的职位，但不知道她干什么好。最后安排她主持早晨脱口秀——《大家谈》，没人知道结果会是什么。

节目取得了极大的成功！经理认为奥普拉天生就是干这个的，奥普拉也这么认为。风趣、机智、热情、魅力四射、富有同情心，她具有了脱口秀主持人所应具备的全部素质。她非常成功，在芝加哥一家更大的电视台主持脱口秀——《早安芝加哥》。一个月内这档节目的收视率就创下了历年的新高。她第二次离开脱口秀主持人位置，转而去拍电影《紫色与本土人》。1985年，她主持的节目更名为《奥普拉秀》，在全美国播放，《奥普拉秀》一跃成为最富人气的电视脱口秀。到了奥普拉·温弗瑞35岁时，她成了是全美国知名度最高的人士之一。

Practising

& Exercise

实战
提升篇

核心单词

possibility [ˌpɔsi'biliti] *n.* 可能性；可能的事

intelligent [in'telidʒənt] *adj.* 有才智的；聪明的；明智的

isolated ['aisəleitid] *adj.* (被)孤立的，(被)分离的，(被)隔离的

behave [bi'heiv] *v.* 表现，行为举止

stepmother ['step‚mʌðə] *n.* 继母，后母

frustration [frʌs'treiʃən] *n.* 挫折，失败，挫败

remove [ri'mu:v] *v.* 移动，搬开；调动

witty ['witi] *adj.* 机智的；诙谐

实用句型

She was so successful that she got a show with a bigger station in Chicago.

她非常成功，在芝加哥更大的一家电视台主持脱口秀。

① so...that 在这里引导结果状语从句。

② successful 成功的，-ful 这个形容词后缀表示"富有……的"，"充满……的"类似的词还有 powerful 有力的，peaceful 和平的；helpful 有帮助的；forgetful 易忘的等。

翻译行不行

1. 这些问题你应该在可行性的报告中提出。(bring up)

....

2. 约翰医生强调不仅要改变饮食还要锻炼身体。(in addition to)

....

3. 他的残忍与犯罪仅距一步之遥。(remove from)

....

If the Dream Is Big Enough
心中有目标，风雨不折腰

· Jack Gates ·

I used to watch her from my kitchen window; she seemed so small as she muscled her way through the crowd of boys on the playground. The school was across the street from our home and I would often watch the kids as they played during **recess**. A sea of children, and yet to me, she stood out from them all.

I remember the first day I saw her playing basketball. I watched in wonder as she ran circles around the other kids. She managed to shoot jump shots just over their heads and into the net. The boys always tried to stop her but no one could.

I began to notice her at other times, basketball in hand, playing alone. She would practice dribbling and shooting over and over again, sometimes until dark. One day I asked her why she practiced so much. She looked directly in my eyes and without a moment of hesitation she said, "I want to go to college. The only way I can go is if I get a scholarship. I like basketball. I decided that if I were good enough, I would get a scholarship. *I am going to play college basketball*. I want to be the best. My Daddy told me if the dream is big enough, the facts don't count. " Then she smiled and ran towards the court to **recap** the **routine** I had seen over and over again.

Well, I had to give it to her—she was determined. I watched her through those junior high years and into high school. Every week, she led her **varsity** team to victory.

One day in her senior year, I saw her sitting in the grass, head cradled in her arms. I walked across the street and sat down in the cool grass beside her. Quietly I asked what was wrong."Oh, nothing," came a soft reply, "I am just too short. " The coach told her that at 5. 5, she would probably never get to play for a top ranked team much less offered a scholarship—so she should stop dreaming about college.

She was heartbroken and I felt my own throat tighten as I sensed her disappointment. I asked her if she had talked to her dad about it yet.

She lifted her head from her hands and told me that her father said those coaches were wrong. They just did not understand the power of a dream. He told her that if she really wanted to play for a good college, if she truly wanted a scholarship, that nothing could stop her except one thing her own **attitude**. He told her again, "If the dream is big enough, the facts don't count. "

The next year, as she and her team went to the Northern California Championship game, she was seen by a college recruiter. She was indeed offered a scholarship, a full ride, to a

Division I, NCAA women's basketball team. She was going to get the college education that she had dreamed of and worked toward for all those years.

It's true: If the dream is big enough, the facts don't count.

杰克·盖茨

我以前常常从厨房的窗户看到她穿梭于操场上的一群男孩子中间，她显得那么矮小。学校在我家的街对面，我可以经常看到孩子们在下课时间打球。操场上有很多孩子，但在我眼里，她依然显得与众人不同。

我记得第一天看到她打篮球的情景。看着她在其他孩子旁边兜来转去，我感到十分惊奇。她总是尽力地跳起投篮，球恰好越过那些孩子的头顶飞入篮筐。那些男孩总是拼命地阻止她，但没有人可以做得到。

我开始注意到她有时候一个人打球。她一遍遍地练习运球和投篮，有时直到天黑。有一天我问她为什么这么刻苦地练习。她直视着我的眼睛，不假思索地说："我想上大学。只有获得奖学金我才能上大学。我喜欢打篮球。我想只要我打得好，我就能获得奖学金。我要到大学去打篮球。我想成为最棒的球员。我爸爸告诉我说，心中有目标，风雨不折腰。"说完她笑了笑，跑向篮球场，又开始我之前见过的一遍又一遍的练习。

嘿，我服了她了——她是下定了决心了。我看着她这些年从初中升到高中。每个星期，她带领的学校篮球代表队都能够获胜。

高中时的某一天，我看见她坐在草地上，头埋在臂弯里。我穿过街道，坐到她旁边的草地上。我轻轻地问出什么事了。"哦，没什么，"她轻声回答，"只是我太矮了。"原来篮球教练告诉她，以五英尺五英寸的身材，她几乎是没有机会到一流的球队去打球的——更不用说会获得奖学金了——所以她应该放弃上大学的梦想。

她很伤心，我也觉得喉咙发紧，因为她的那种失望我也能感同身受。我问她是否与她的爸爸谈过这件事。

她从臂弯里抬起头，告诉我，她爸爸说那些教练错了。他们根本不懂得梦想的力量。他告诉她，如果真的想到一个好的大学去打篮球，如果她真的想获得奖学金，任何东西都不能阻止她，除非她自己不愿意。他又一次跟她说："心中有目标，风雨不折腰。"

第二年，当她和她的球队去参加北加利福尼亚州冠军赛时，她被一位大学的招生人员看中了。她真的获得了奖学金，而且还是全额奖学金，并且进入了全国大学体育协会中的一队——女子甲组篮球队。在那里，她将开始她曾梦想并为之奋斗多年的大学生活。

是的，心中有目标，风雨不折腰。

核心单词

recess [ri'ses] *n.* 休息；休会；学校的假期

recap ['ri:kæp] *n.* 重述要点　*v.* 扼要重述；概括

routine [ru:'ti:n] *n.* 例行公事；惯例

varsity ['vɑ:siti] *n.* 大学；大学代表队

attitude ['ætitju:d] *n.* 态度，意见，看法

实用句型

I am going to play college basketball. 我要到大学去打篮球。

① 用 "be going to" 表示将来上大学是经过事先考虑好的。

② play basketball 打篮球；类似的表达还有 play volleyball 排球；play table tennis 乒乓球；play hockey 曲棍球；play tennis 网球；play badminton 羽毛球；但在乐器前要加 the，如 play the piano 弹钢琴。

翻译行不行

1. 天安门广场上人山人海。(a sea of)

....

2. 他们毫不犹豫地就同意了。(without a moment of hesitation)

....

3. 孩子们好奇地盯着魔术师。(in wonder)

....

The Master of Investment: Warren Buffett
世界投资大师：沃伦·巴菲特

· Alfred ·

For someone who is such an extraordinarily successful investor, Warren Buffett comes off as a pretty ordinary guy. Born and bred in Omaha, Nebraska, for more than 40 years Buffett has lived in the same gray stucco house on Farnam Street that he bought for $31, 500. He wears **rumpled**, nondescript suits, drives his own car, drinks Cherry Coke, and is more likely to be found in a Dairy Queen than a four-star restaurant.

But the 68-year-old Omaha native has led an extraordinary life. Looking back on his childhood, one can see the budding of a savvy businessman. Warren Edward Buffett was born on August 30, 1930, the middle child of three. His father, Howard Buffett, came from a family of grocers but himself became a stockbroker and later a U. S. congressman.

Even as a young child, Buffett was pretty serious about making money. He used to go door-to-door and sell soda pop. He and a friend used math to develop a system for picking winners in horseracing and started selling their "Stable-Boy Selections" tip sheets until they were shut down for not having a license. Later, he also worked at his grandfather's grocery store. At the ripe age of 11, Buffett bought his first stock.

When his family moved to Washington D. C. , Buffett became a paperboy for *The Washington Post* and its rival the *Times-Herald*. Buffett ran his five paper routes like an **assembly** line and even added magazines to round out his product offerings. While still in school, he was making $175 a month, a **full-time** wage for many young men.

When he was 14, Buffett spent $1, 200 on 40 acres of farmland in Nebraska and soon began collecting rent from a tenant farmer. He and a friend also made $50 a week by placing pinball machines in barber shops. They called their venture Wilson Coin Operated Machine Co.

Already a successful albeit small-time businessman, Buffett wasn't keen on going to college but ended up at Wharton at the University of Pennsylvania—his father encouraged him to go. After two years at Wharton, Buffett transferred to his parents' alma mater, the University of Nebraska in Lincoln, for his final year of college. There Buffett took a job with the *Lincoln Journal* supervising 50 paper boys in six rural counties.

Buffett applied to Harvard Business School but was turned down in what had to be one of the worst admissions decisions in Harvard history. The outcome ended up profoundly affecting Buffett's life, for he ended up attending Columbia Business School, where he studied under revered mentor Benjamin Graham, the father of securities **analysis** who provided the foundation for Buffett's investment strategy.

From the beginning, Buffett made his **fortune** from investing. He started with all the money he had made from selling pop, delivering papers, and operating pinball machines. Between 1950 and 1956, he grew his $9, 800 kitty to $14, 000. From there, he organized investment partnerships with his family and friends, and then gradually drew in other investors through word of mouth and very attractive terms.

Buffett's goal was to top the **Dow Jones Industrial Average** by an average of 10% a year. Over the length of the Buffett partnership between 1957 and 1969, Buffett's investments grew at a compound **annual** rate of 29.5%, crushing the Dow's return of 7.4% over the same period.

Buffett's investment strategy mirrors his lifestyle and overall philosophy. He doesn't collect houses or cars or works of art, and he disdains companies that waste money on such extravagances as limousines, private dining rooms, and high-priced real estate. He is a creature of habit—same house, same office, same city, same soda—and dislikes change. In his investments, that means holding on to "core holdings" such as American Express, Coca-Cola, and The Washington Post Co. "forever."

Buffett's view of inherited money also departs from the norm. Critical of the self-indulgence of the super-rich, Buffett thinks of inheritances as "privately funded food stamps" that keep children of the rich from leading normal, independent lives. With his own three kids, he gave them each $10, 000 a year— the tax-deductible limit—at Christmas. When he gave them a loan, they had to sign a written agreement. When his daughter, also named Susie like her mother, needed $20 to park at the airport, he made her write him a check for it.

As for charity, Buffett's strict standards have made it difficult for him to give much away. He evaluates charities the same way he looks for stocks : value for money, return on invested capital. He has established the Buffett Foundation, designed to **accumulate** money and give it away after his and his wife's deaths—though the foundation has given millions to organizations involved with population control, family planning, abortion, and birth control. The argument goes that Buffett can actually give away a greater sum in the end by growing his money while he's still **alive**.

One thing's for sure about Buffett—He's happy doing what he's doing. "I get to do what I like to do every single day of the year," he says. "I get to do it with people I like, and I don't have to associate with anybody who causes my stomach to churn. I tap dance to work, and when I get there I think I'm supposed to lie on my back and paint the ceiling. It's tremendous fun." It's fun to watch the master at work, too.

阿尔弗雷德

作为一个如此卓越的成功投资家，沃伦·巴菲特却又是一个非常平凡、普通的人。巴菲特在美国内布拉斯加州的奥马哈出生、长大，40 多年来他一直居住的是法钠姆大街那栋自己以 31 500 美元购置的灰色水泥墙的房子。他穿皱巴巴的普通西装，亲自开车，常喝"樱桃可乐"，多数情况下是光顾"DQ"这样的小馆，而不是四星级的豪华酒店。

但这位 68 岁、土生土长的奥马哈人却有着不平凡的生活经历。回顾他的童年时代，就可以很好地了解这个机敏的生意人的成长过程。沃伦·爱德华·巴菲特生于 1930 年 8 月 30 日，在家里 3 个孩子中排行老二。他父亲霍华德·巴菲特成长于一个杂货商的家庭中，但后来却成了一名股票经纪人，之后又成为美国国会的议员。

甚至在很小的时候，巴菲特就对赚钱很用心。那时他常常挨家挨户地推销苏打汽水。他和一个朋友利用数学知识开发了一个在赛马比赛中选拔冠军的识别系统，然后开始推销他们的"马童筛选器"的内部消息传单，但因为无许可证被迫关停。后来他还在祖父的杂货店干过一段时间。在 11 岁的时候，已近成熟的巴菲特买进了自己的第一支股票。

在巴菲特全家搬至华盛顿后，他开始为《华盛顿邮报》和该报的对手《时代先驱报》送报纸。巴菲特把自己送报的 5 条线路安排得就像生产线一样有条不紊，后来他甚至还添加了杂志的递送，这样他提供的订阅品种就更丰富了。在校读书期间，他每月的收入就已经有 175 美元了，相当于当时年轻人全职工作的月收入。

14 岁那年，巴菲特花了 1 200 美元在内布拉斯加州购置了一片 40 公顷的农田，然后开始从佃户那里收取租金。他还和一个朋友为理发店安装弹球游戏机从而每周赚得 50 美元。他们把自己的"企业"称作"威尔森钱币运作机器公司"。

这时巴菲特尽管并不起眼,但已是一个小获成功的商人。他对上大学并不感兴趣,不过后来还是在父亲的敦促下去了宾夕法尼亚大学的沃顿学院。在沃顿学习了两年后,巴菲特转学到其父母的母校——内布拉斯加大学的林肯分校,在那儿修完了大学最后一年的课程。这期间巴菲特还在《林肯日报》谋得了一份工作,负责管理6个乡村地区的50个报童。

巴菲特曾申请哈佛商学院被拒,这后来成为哈佛历史上最糟糕的录取决定之一。这个结果对巴菲特的一生产生了深远的影响,他因此进入哥伦比亚商学院,并师从著名的证券分析之父本杰明·格雷厄姆,巴菲特从导师身上学到的东西为日后形成自己的投资策略奠定了基础。

一开始,巴菲特凭借投资来赚钱。他最初的资本来自卖苏打汽水、送报纸、安装弹球游戏机而攒下的积蓄。在1950到1956年期间,他的原始资本积累由9 800美元升至14 000美元。此后,巴菲特开始与家人和朋友结成伙伴投资关系,后来又凭借口头游说和一些优惠条件拉拢其他投资者。

巴菲特的目的是以每年平均10%的比率超出道琼斯工业指数。在巴菲特倡导的"合伙投资"模式下,从1957到1969年间,巴菲特的投资以每年29.5%的综合速度增长,大大挫败了道琼斯在同一时期7.4%的回报率。

巴菲特的投资策略可映射出他的生活方式和人生哲学。他没有囤积房屋、收集汽车和艺术品的嗜好,他厌恶那些把钱花在高级轿车、私人餐厅和豪华地产这类奢侈品上的公司。他是个善于遵循习惯的人——住同一栋房屋,在同一间办公室办公,在同一个城市生活，喝同一牌子的可乐——他不喜欢变化。用在他的投资理念上，就是紧抓住投资"核心"不变，如美国捷运公司、可口可乐、华盛顿邮报公司，而且是"永远不变"。

巴菲特对待遗产的态度也与众不同。他对"超级富人"自我放纵的生活方式非常反感，他把遗产看作是"私人资助的饭票"，这让有钱人家的孩子们无法过上正常而独立的生活。对自己的3个孩子，巴菲特在每年圣诞节时给他们每人1万美元作为一年的花销——免征所得税收的最低限度。若是给他们贷款，则需签订书面协议。有一次他的女儿苏茜——与母亲同名——在机场需要20美元的停车费，巴菲特虽然把钱借给了她，但却要求女儿给自己写一张支票当作偿还。

巴菲特严格的处事标准使他即使是面对慈善事业也很难慷慨解囊。他对待慈善事业的态度犹如对待股票：认真评估投入资本的有价回报。他建立了巴菲特基金会，意在积累资金，在自己和妻子死后发放。不过巴菲特基金会至今已为许多组织捐资数百万美元，资助的项目包括人口控制、计划生育、堕胎和避孕等。许多人认为通过进一步扩张现有财力，巴菲特在有生之年就可最终捐出一大笔款项。

对于巴菲特来说，有一点是可以肯定的：他非常热爱自己的工作。"一年中的每一天我都在做自己喜欢做的事，我与自己喜欢的人一起工作。我用不着与自己讨厌的人打交道。我欣然扑向工作，到了公司我会觉得工作就好像是让自己仰面躺下，用手中的笔绘制天花板一般轻松。工作让我乐趣无穷。"巴菲特说。当然，看一位大师级人物工作也同样是乐趣无穷。

核心单词

rumpled ['rʌmpld] *adj.* 弄皱的；凌乱的

assembly [ə'sembli] *n.* 集会；集合

full-time ['ful'taim] *adj.* 专任的；全日制的

analysis [ə'nælisis] *n.* 分析；分解；解析

fortune [fɔ:tʃ ne] *n.* 财产，财富；巨款

Dow Jones Industrial Average 道琼斯工业指数

annual ['ænjuəl] *adj.* 一年一次的；每年的；全年的

accumulate [ə'kju:mjuleit] *v.* 累积，积聚；积攒

alive [ə'laiv] *adj.* 活着的；现存的

实用句型

As for charity, Buffett's strict standards have made it difficult for him to give much away.

巴菲特严格的处事标准使他即使是面对慈善事业也很难慷慨解囊。

①介词短语 as for charity 在句中做状语。

② give away 赠送，分发，类似的表达还有 give out 分发，用尽；give in 让步，呈交；give up 让出，放弃等固定搭配。

翻译行不行

1. 想起过去，我仍然不寒而栗。(look back on)

....

2. 公司在夏天会放三个星期的假。(shut down)

....

3. 我认为这是不可能的。(think of)

....

If I Were a Boy Again
假如我重返少年

• Anonymous •

If I were a boy again, I would **cultivate** courage. "Nothing is so mild and gentle as courage, nothing so cruel and pitiless as cowardice. " says a wise author. We too often borrow trouble, and **anticipate** that that may never appear. "The fear of ill exceeds the ill we fear. " Dangers will **arise** in any career, but the presence of mind will often conquer the worst of them. Be prepared for any fate, and there is no harm to be feared.

If I were a boy again, I would look on the cheerful side. Life is very much like a mirror: if you smile upon it, it smiles back upon you ; but if you **frown** and look doubtful on it, you will get a similar look in return. Inner sunshine warms not only the heart of the owner, but of all that come in contact with it. "Who shuts love out, in turn shall be shut out from love. "

If I were a boy again, I would school myself to say "no" more often. I might write pages on the importance of learning very early in life to gain that point where a young boy can stand **erect**, and decline doing an unworthy act because it is unworthy.

If I were a boy again, I would demand of myself more

courtesy towards my companions and friends, and indeed towards strangers as well. The smallest courtesies along the rough roads of life are like the little birds that sing to us all winter long, and make that season of ice and snow more **endurable**.

Finally, instead of trying hard to be happy, as if that were the solepurpose of life, I would, if I were a boy again, I would still try harder tomake others happy.

佚　名

假如我重返少年，我就要培养勇气。一位明智的作家曾说过："世上没有东西比勇气更温文尔雅，也没有东西比懦怯更残酷无情。"我们常常过多地自寻烦恼，杞人忧天。"怕祸害比祸害本身更可怕。"凡事都有危险，但镇定沉着往往能克服最严重的危险。对一切祸福做好准备，那么就没有什么灾难可以害怕的了。

假如我重返少年，我就要事事乐观。生活犹如一面镜子：你朝它笑，它也朝你笑；如果你双眉紧锁，向它投以怀疑的目光，它也将还以你同样的目光。内心的欢乐不仅温暖了欢乐者自己的心，也温暖了所有与之接触者的心。"谁拒爱于门外，也必将被爱拒之门外。"

假如我重返少年，我就要养成经常说"不"字的习惯。一个少年要能挺得起腰，拒绝做不应该做的事，就因为这事不值得做。我可以写上好几页谈谈早年培养这一点的重要性。

假如我重返少年，我就要要求自己对伙伴和朋友更加礼貌，而且对陌生人也应如此。在坎坷的生活道路上，最细小的礼貌犹如在漫长的冬天为我们歌唱的小鸟，那歌声使冰天雪地的寒冬变得较易忍受。

最后，假如我重返少年，我不会力图为自己谋幸福，好像这就是人生唯一的目的；与之相反，我要更努力地为他人谋幸福。

核心单词

cultivate ['kʌltiveit] v. 耕种，培养；陶冶

anticipate [æn'tisipeit] v. 预期，期望；预料

arise [ə'raiz] v. 升起，上升；产生

frown [fraun] v. 皱眉；表示不满

erect [i'rekt] adj. 直立的，垂直的   v. 使竖立，使竖直

courtesy ['kə:tisi] n. 礼貌；殷勤，好意

endurable [in'djuərəbl] adj. 能持久的；耐用的；可忍受的

实用句型

If I were a boy again, I would look on the cheerful side.

假如我重返少年，我就要事事乐观。

①这句话用的是虚拟语气，说明与现在事实相反的情况。

② look on 面向，看待，类似的表达还有 look up 查询；look for 寻找；look over 仔细检查；look into 研究，调查等固定搭配。

翻译行不行

1. 他以优良的成绩作为对妈妈辛勤劳作的回报。(in return)

....

2. 你现在与他有联系吗？（in contact with）

....

3. 这位护士不仅能干而且亲切和蔼。(not only...but also)

....

Frederic Francois Chopin

钢琴诗人——肖邦

• Derek •

Frederic Francois Chopin, Polish-born composer and renowned pianist, was the creator of 55 mazurkas, 13 polonaises, 24 preludes, 27 etudes, 19 nocturnes, 4 ballads, and 4 scherzos.

Frederic Chopin was born in Zelazowa Wola, Poland, on February 22, 1810, to a French father and Polish mother. His father, Nicholas Chopin, was a French **tutor** to many aristocratic Polish families, later accepting a position as a French teacher at the Warsaw Lyceum.

Although Chopin later attended the Lyceum where his father taught, his early training began at home. This included receiving piano lessons from his mother. By the age of six, Chopin was creating original pieces, showing **innate prodigious** musical ability. His parents arranged for the young Chopin to take piano instruction from Wojciech Zywny.

When Chopin was sixteen, he **attended** the Warsaw Conservatory of Music, **directed** by composer Joseph Elsner. Elsner, like Zywny, insisted on the traditional training associated with Classical music but allowed his students to investigate the more original imaginations of the Romantic style as well.

As often happened with the young musicians of both the Classical and Romantic Periods, Chopin was sent to Vienna, the unquestioned center of music for that day. He gave piano concerts and then arranged to have his pieces published by a Viennese publishing house there. While Chopin was in Austria, Poland and Russia faced off in the **apparent** beginnings of war. He returned to Warsaw to get his things in preparation of a more permanent move. While there, his friends gave him a silver goblet filled with Polish soil. He kept it always, as he was never able to return to his beloved Poland.

French by **heritage**, and desirous of finding musical acceptance from a less traditional audience than that of Vienna, Chopin ventured to Paris. Interestingly, other young musicians had assembled in the city of fashion with the very same hope. Chopin joined Franz Liszt, Hector Berlioz, Felix Mendelssohn, Vincenzo Bellini, and Auguste Franchomme, all proponents of the "new" Romantic style.

Although Chopin did play in the large concert halls on occasion, he felt most at home in private settings, enjoying the social milieu that accompanied concerts for the wealthy. He also enjoyed teaching, as this caused him less stress than performing. Chopin did not feel that his delicate technique and **intricate** melodies were as suited to the grandiose hall as they were to smaller environments and audiences.

News of the war in Poland inspired Chopin to write many sad

musical pieces expressing his grief for "his" Poland. Among these was the famous *Revolutionary Etude*. **Plagued** by poor health as well as his homesickness, Chopin found solace in summer visits to the country. Here, his most complex yet harmonic creations found their way to the brilliant composer's hand. The *Fantasia in F Minor*, the *Barcarolle*, the *Polonaise Fantasia*, *Ballade in A Flat Major*, *Ballade in F Minor*, and Sonata in B Minor were all products of the relaxed time Chopin enjoyed in the country.

As the war continued in Warsaw and then reached Paris, Chopin retired to Scotland with friends. Although he was far beyond the reach of the revolution, his melancholy attitude did not improve and he sank deeper into a depression. Likewise, his health did not rejuvenate either. A window in the fighting made it possible for Chopin to return to Paris as his health deteriorated further. Surrounded by those that he loved, Frederic Francois Chopin died at the age of 39. He was buried in Paris.

Chopin's last request was that the Polish soil in the silver goblet be sprinkled over his grave.

德里克

肖邦,波兰籍作曲家,也是著名的钢琴家。他一生创作了55部马祖卡舞曲,13部波罗涅兹,24首序曲,27首练习曲,

19 首夜曲，4 首叙事曲，以及 4 部诙谐曲。

1810 年 2 月 12 日，肖邦出生于波兰华沙郊区的热拉佐瓦沃拉。他的父亲尼古拉斯是法国人，而母亲却是一位地道的波兰人。尼古拉斯原本是波兰贵族家庭的一名法语教师，后来到华沙的一所中学教授法语。

尽管肖邦后来到父亲所教授的学校学习，但他最初的音乐训练来自家庭。六岁那年，肖邦创作出了人生的第一部作品，充分展现了他与生俱来的非凡的音乐天赋。不久后，他进入了父亲所在的学校学习，并在父母的安排下，跟随捷克音乐家 W・日夫尼学习钢琴。

16 岁时，肖邦进入华沙音乐学院学习，师从音乐家约瑟夫・埃尔斯纳。与日尼夫相同的是，埃尔斯纳在坚持古典派推崇的传统练习外，鼓励学生们从浪漫派中吸取灵感。

像许多兼古典和浪漫于一身的年轻音乐家一样，肖邦在离开华沙音乐学院后，来到了当时的音乐圣地——维也纳。在那里，肖邦不仅举行了多场音乐会，也发表了不少音乐作品。在波兰民族运动走向高潮，与沙俄的战争一触即发的时候，肖邦身在奥地利。不久，他回到华沙为出国做准备。临行前，华沙音乐学院的师生们为他送行，并赠以盛满祖国泥土的银杯。尽管从此肖邦再也没有回到他深爱着的祖国，他一直保存着这捧祖国的泥土。

为了得到更多浪漫派听众的认可，加上自己拥有一半的法国血统，肖邦来到了法国巴黎。有趣的是，许多抱有同样想法的年轻音乐家们也都聚集到了这座流行之都。在这里，肖邦结识了西欧文艺界许多重要人物，包括匈牙利艺术家李斯特，柏辽兹，门德尔松，意大利音乐家贝利尼，奥古斯特·弗朗肖姆等新浪漫主义的拥护者。

尽管肖邦有时也在大型音乐厅演出，但他更喜欢在家或是一些私人的场合，享受更融洽的氛围。他也更喜欢教学时放松的心情。肖邦认为他细致优美的演奏技巧和纷繁的旋律更适合小环境演奏，而不适合宏伟的音乐厅。

波兰陷入战火的消息促使他写了许多充满悲伤的作品，以表达对祖国波兰的哀伤与思念，其中包括名曲《革命练习曲》。肖邦的健康状况一直不佳，加上思乡心切，一度患上肺病，曾在法国南部疗养。期间写过不少成名的珍品。《F 小调幻想曲》，《威尼斯船歌》，《幻想波罗涅兹舞曲》，《降 A 大调叙事曲》，《F 小调叙事曲》，《B 小调奏鸣曲》等都是在南部疗养时创作的。

战事从华沙蔓延到了巴黎，肖邦不得不和朋友们躲避至苏格兰。虽然肖邦远离了波兰的战火，但他忧郁的情绪丝毫没有改善，反而陷入了更深的沮丧之中。同样地，他的健康状况也没有恢复。回巴黎后，肖邦的健康状况急剧下降，最终在友人们的陪伴下逝世于巴黎的寓所中，结束了短短 39 年的生命。他的遗体被安葬在巴黎。

肖邦最后的遗愿是将银杯中的祖国波兰的泥土撒在他的坟墓上。

核心单词

tutor ['tju:tə] *n.* 家庭教师，私人教师

innate ['ineit] *adj.* 与生俱来的；天生的；固有的

prodigious [prə'didʒəs] *adj.* 巨大的；庞大的

attend [ə'tend] *v.* 出席，参加

directed [di'rektid] *adj.* 经指导的；应用的

apparent [ə'pærənt] *adj.* 表面的，外观的；未必真实的

heritage ['heritidʒ] *n.* 遗产，继承物；遗留物

intricate ['intrikit] *adj.* 错综复杂的；复杂精细的

plague [pleig] *n.* 天灾，灾难，祸患

实用句型

Although Chopin later attended the Lyceum where his father taught，his early training began at home. 尽管肖邦后来到父亲所教授的学校学习，但他最初的音乐训练来自家庭。

①这里是 although 引导的让步状语从句。

②attend 出席，参加，类似的表达还有 join in；take part in；participate in 等固定搭配。

翻译行不行

1. 他出生在中国。(be born in)

....

2. 计划我已安排好了。(arrange for)

....

3. 中国是煤炭生产大国，同时其他的矿藏也非常丰富。(as well)

....

An Exhausting Struggle
一场累人的斗争

· Frank ·

Balzac once said **artistic** creation was "an exhausting struggle". *He believed that only by tenacious work and not being afraid of difficulties could you show your talent*. It was just like the soldiers charging the fortress, not **relaxing** your effort even for a moment.

Once Balzac wrote for hours on end, he was so tired that he could not hold out any longer. He ran to a friend's home and plunged headlong onto the sofa. He wanted to sleep, but he told his friend he must be woken up within an hour. His friend, seeing him so tired, did not wake him up on time. After he woke up, Balzac got very angry at his friend. Fortunately his friend had an **intimate** understanding of him and did not quarrel with him.

Balzac did not smoke cigarettes, nor did he drink any alcohol. But he got one habit : while he was writing he always drank very strong coffee that could almost anaesthetize his stomach. He didn't add milk, nor did he add sugar in his coffee. It would not **satisfy** him until it was made bitter. People generally did not like to drink such bitter coffee. That had a strange **stimulus** effect on him, and could help him drive the sleepiness away, according to himself.

弗兰克

巴尔扎克曾经说过，艺术创造是"一场累人的斗争"。他认为，只有顽强地工作，不怕困难，才能把自己的才华表现出来。这就好像向堡垒冲击的战士，一刻也不能松劲。

有一次，巴尔扎克一连写了好几个小时，累得实在支持不住了，跑到一个朋友家里，一头倒在沙发上。他想睡一觉，但他告诉朋友，一定要在一小时之内叫醒他。他的朋友见他非常疲劳，就没有按时叫醒他。他醒来后，对朋友大发脾气。幸好他的朋友很了解他，没有和他争吵。

巴尔扎克既不抽烟，也不喝酒。但他有个习惯：当他写作的时候，总是呷着几乎可以使胃麻痹的浓咖啡。他的咖啡里既不加牛奶，也不加糖，要熬得发苦才满意。像这样苦的咖啡，一般人都不愿意喝。但他却认为，这样对他有奇异的刺激作用，可以驱走睡魔。

核心单词

exhausting [ig'zɔːstiŋ] *adj.* 使耗尽的；使人精疲力竭的

artistic [ɑːˈtistik] *adj.* 艺术的；美术的；唯美（主义）的

relaxing [riˈlæksiŋ] *adj.* 令人松懈的，轻松愉悦的

intimate [ˈintimit] *adj.* 亲密的，熟悉的

satisfy [ˈsætisfai] *v.* 使满意，使高兴；使满足

stimulus [ˈstimjuləs] *n.* 刺激；刺激品；兴奋剂

实用句型

He believed that only by tenacious work and not being afraid of difficulties could you show your talent.

他认为，只有顽强工作，不怕困难，才能把自己的才华表现出来。

①这是用 that 引导的宾语从句。

② afraid of 害怕，类似的表达还有 afraid to 不敢（做）等固定搭配。

翻译行不行

1. 他不在这儿住了。(not... any longer)

....

2. 他连续几个月都在写他的小说。(on end)

....

3. 他将据其罪行的轻重受到处罚。(according to)

....

The Greatest American Athlete
美国最伟大的运动员

• Gaby •

The railroad station was **jammed**. Students from Lafayette College were crowding onto the train platform **eagerly** awaiting the arrival of the Carlisle Indian School's track and field squad. No one would have believed it a few months earlier. *A school that nobody had heard of was suddenly beating big, famous colleges in track meets*. Surely these Carlisle athletes would come charging off the train, one after another, like a Marine battalion.

The train finally arrived and two young men—one big and broad, the other small and slight—stepped onto the platform.

"Where is the track team?" a Lafayette student asked.

"This is the team," **replied** the big fellow.

"Just the two of you?"

"Nope, just me," said the big fellow. "This little guy is the manager."

The Lafayette students shook their heads in wonder. Somebody must be playing a joke on them. If this big fellow was the whole Carlisle track team, he would be competing against an **entire** Lafayette squad.

He did. He ran sprints, he ran hurdles, he ran distance races.

He high-jumped, he broad-jumped. He threw the javelin and the shot. Finishing first in eight events, the big fellow beat the whole Lafayette team.

The big fellow was Jim Thorpe, the greatest American athlete of modern times.

加 比

火车站挤得水泄不通。拉斐德学院的学生们一齐拥上站台，热切地等待着卡莱尔印第安人学校田径队的到来。倘若在几个月前，准没有人相信，一个谁也没听说过的学校，会在田径场上突然大败许多有名的大学。不用说，这些卡莱尔的运动员抵达后，准会像一营海军陆战队队员那样，一个接一个冲下火车。

火车终于到站了，两个年轻人——一位，个儿高，体态魁梧；另一位，个儿矮，长相瘦弱——踏上了站台。

"田径队在哪儿？"一位拉斐德的学生问道。

"就在这儿，"大个子回答道。

"就你们两个？"

"不，就我一个，"大个子说。"这位小兄弟是领队。"

拉斐德的学生们诧异地摇摇头。一定有人在和他们开玩笑。如果卡莱尔田径队就只有大个子一人，那他就得和整个拉斐德田径队比试高低了。

确实如此。他短跑、跨栏、长跑、跳高、跳远。他又投标枪又掷铅球。大个子赢得八项第一，一个人击败了整个拉斐德田径队。

这位大个子就是美国现代最伟大的运动员吉姆·索普。

Practising

& Exercise

核心单词

jammed ['dʒæmd] *adj.* 卡住的；拥挤的；堵塞的

eagerly ['i:gəli] *adv.* 渴望地；热切地

reply [ri'plai] *v.* 回答，答复

entire [in'taiə] *adj.* 全部的，整个的

实用句型

A school that nobody had heard of was suddenly beating big，famous colleges in track meets.

一个谁也没听说过的学校，会在田径场上突然大败许多有名的大学。

①这里是 that 引导的定语从句，修饰限定 a school。

② hear of 听说，类似的表达还有 hear from 接到……的信，受……批评；hear about 听说，接到消息等固定搭配。

翻译行不行

1. 她把错误归咎于缺乏经验。(charge off)

....

2. 我们赢得了一个又一个的胜利。(one after another)

....

3. 这个国家在贸易方面正与其他国家竞争。(compete against)

....

George Soros—the Financial Crocodile
金融大鳄乔治·索罗斯

· James ·

George Soros wants to be the Bono of the financial world. The speculator whose assault on sterling ejected Britain from the European exchange rate mechanism that September of 10 years ago has a mission—to use his estimated $5 bn fortune and his fame to help **tackle** what he sees as the failures of globalization. The idea that a man who made billions betting on the financial markets sides with the anti-globalization movement might strike some as ironic. Soros is clearly genuinely appalled at the damage wrought on vulnerable economies by the vast sums of money which flow across national borders every day.

"The US governs the international system to protect its own economy. It is not in charge of protecting other economies," he says. "So when America goes into recession, you have anti-recessionary policies. When other countries are in recession, they don't have the ability to engage in anti-recessionary policies because they can't have a permissive monetary policy, because money would flee." In person, he has the air of a philosophy professor rather than a gimlet-eyed financier. In a soft voice which bears the traces of his native Hungary, he argues that it is time to rewrite the so-called Washington consensus—the cocktail of liberalization, privatization and fiscal rectitude which the IMF has been preaching for 15 years. Developing countries no longer have the freedom to run their own economies, he argues, even when they follow **perfectly** sound policies. He cites Brazil, which although it has a floating currency and manageable public debt was paying ten times over the **odds** to borrow from capital markets.

Soros, who at one stage after the fall of the Berlin Wall was providing more assistance to Russia than the US government, believes in practising what he preaches. His Open Society Institute has been **pivotal** in helping eastern European countries develop democratic societies and market economies. Soros has the advantage of an insider's knowledge of the workings of global capitalism, so his criticism is particularly pointed. Last year, the Soros foundation's network spent nearly half a billion dollars on projects in education, public health and promoting democracy, making it one of the world's largest private donors.

Soros credits the anti-globalization movement for having made companies more sensitive to their wider responsibilities. "I think (the protesters) have made an important contribution by making people aware of the flaws of the system,"he says."people on the street had an impact on public opinion and corporations which sell to the public responded to that." Because the IMF has abandoned billion dollar bailouts for troubled economies, he thinks a repeat of the Asian crisis is unlikely. The fund's new "tough love" policy—for which Argentina is the guinea pig — has other consequences. The bailouts were a welfare system for Wall Street, with western taxpayers **rescuing** the banks from the consequences of unwise lending to emerging economies. *Now the IMF has drawn a line in the sand, credit to poor countries is drying up.* "It has created a new problem—the inadequacy of the flow of capital from centre to the periphery," he says.

詹姆士

乔治·索罗斯想成为金融界的博诺（U2 乐队主唱）。这位在 10 年前的那个 9 月份攻击英镑迫使英国退出欧洲汇率机制的投机商有一项使命——利用他大约 50 亿英镑的财产和他的名声来帮助解决他所认为的全球化失败问题。一个靠在全球金融市场上的投机赚了几十亿的人会支持反全球化运动，这对许多人来说是具有讽刺意义的。很明显，对于每天在各国之间流动的大量资金给经济脆弱国家造成的伤害，索罗斯从心底感到震惊。

索罗斯说："美国管理国际经济体系是为了保护本国利益，它并不负责保护其他国家的经济。因此，当美国陷入衰退后，美国会出台反衰退政策。而其他国家陷入衰退时，却无力这样做，因为这些国家不能实行自由开放的金融政策，否则资金就会外流。"索罗斯本人并不像一个目光敏锐的金融家，他更具有哲学教授的气质。带着匈牙利母语口音，他轻声地说，现在是修改所谓的"华盛顿共识"的时侯了。他指的是国际货币基金组织 15 年来宣扬的自由化、私有化和财政透明的综合体制。他说，发展中国家即使执行非常合理的政策，也不能自由地控制本国经济了。他援引巴西的例子说，尽管巴西实行了浮动汇率制和可控国债，但它向资本市场借款还是付出了比正常条件下高出 10 倍的成本。

索罗斯在柏林墙倒塌后一段时间内向俄罗斯提供的援助曾一度超过美国政府的援助。他坚定地实施自己宣扬的观点。他的"开放社会研究所"在帮助东欧国家发展民主社会和市场经济方面发挥了重要作用。索罗斯具有业内人士的优势，了解全球资本主义的运行，因此他的批评会受到特别关注。去年索罗斯基金网络在教育、公共卫生、促进民主项目上花费了近 5 亿美元，使索罗斯基金成为世界上最大的私人捐助集团之一。

索罗斯赞扬反全球化运动使各公司更加认识到自己更广泛的责任。他说："我认为（反对者们）作出了重要贡献，使大众意识到这个体系的缺陷。大街上的人们对舆论会有所影响，而向公众推销商品的公司也会对舆论作出反应。"由于国际货币基金组织已经拒绝向经济困难的国家提供数十亿美元的救济，索罗斯认为亚洲经济危机不会重演。国际货币基金组织"既爱又严"的新政策——阿根廷是该政策的试验品——带来了其他后果。西方纳税人挽救了银行因不理智地向新兴国家提供贷款造成的恶果，而国际货币基金组织的那些救济金则成了华尔街的福利制度。现在国际货币基金组织对贫困国家的贷款正在枯竭。索罗斯说："这就产生了一个新问题——资金从中心向周边流动不足。"

灰色晨曦中，那通往彩虹的路

221

Practising
& Exercise

实战
提升篇

核心单词

tackle ['tækl] *v.* 着手对付（或处理）；与……交涉

perfectly ['pɜ:fiktli] *adv.* 完美地；圆满地；完全地

odds [ɔds] *n.* 机会，可能性；成功的可能性

pivotal ['pivətl] *adj.* 中枢的；重要的

rescue ['reskju:] *v.* 援救；营救；挽救

实用句型

Now the IMF has drawn a line in the sand, credit to poor countries is drying up. 现在国际货币基金组织对贫困国家的贷款正在枯竭。

① has drawn 是现在完成时的表达方式，have/has +done。

② dry up 干涸，类似的表达还有 dry out 干透；dry off 变干等固定搭配。

翻译行不行

1. 经理不在时，他负责这个商店。(in charge of)

....

2. 救生艇被派出去救沉船的水手了。(rescue from)

....

3. 主办国本身也因外来人才的到来而获益匪浅。(benefit from)

....